FAMILY AND HOUSEHOLD I

Social History in Perspective
General Editor: Jeremy Black

Social History in Perspective is a series of in-depth studies of the many topics in social, cultural and religious history for students. They also give the student clear surveys of the subject and present the most recent research in an accessible way.

PUBLISHED

John Belchem *Popular Radicalism in Nineteenth-Century Britain*
Sue Bruley *Women in Britain since 1900*
Simon Dentith *Society and Cultural Forms in Nineteenth-Century England*
Peter Fleming *Family and Household in Medieval England*
Harry Goulbourne *Race Relations in Britain since 1945*
Tim Hitchcock *English Sexualities, 1700–1800*
Sybil M. Jack *Towns in Tudor and Stuart Britain*
Helen M. Jewell *Education in Early Modern England*
Alan Kidd *State, Society and the Poor in Nineteenth-Century England*
Arthur J. McIver *A History of Work in Britain, 1880–1950*
Hugh McLeod *Religion and Society in England, 1850–1914*
Donald M. MacRaild *Irish Migrants in Modern Britain, 1750–1922*
Donald R. MacRaild and David E. Martin *Labour in British Society, 1830–1914*
Christopher Marsh *Popular Religion in the Sixteenth Century*
Michael A. Mullett *Catholics in Britain and Ireland, 1558–1829*
Malcolm Smuts *Culture and Power in England, 1585–1685*
John Spurr *English Puritanism, 1603–1689*
W. B. Stephens *Education in Britain, 1750–1914*
Heather Swanson *Medieval British Towns*
David Taylor *Crime, Policing and Punishment in England, 1750–1914*
N. L. Tranter *British Populations in the Twentieth Century*
Ian D. Whyte *Migration and Society in Britain, 1550–1830*
Ian D. Whyte *Scotland's Society and Economy in Transition, c.1500–c.1760*

Please note that a sister series, *British History in Perspective*, is available which covers all the key topics in British political history.

Social History in Perspective
Series Standing Order
ISBN 0–333–71694–9 hardcover
ISBN 0–333–69336–1 paperback
(outside North America only)

You can receive future titles in this series as they are published by placing a standing order. Please contact your bookseller or, in the case of difficulty, write to us at the addresss below with your name and address, the title of the series and the ISBN quoted above.

Customer Services Department, Macmillan Distribution Ltd

FAMILY AND HOUSEHOLD IN MEDIEVAL ENGLAND

Peter Fleming

palgrave

First published 2001 by
PALGRAVE
Houndmills, Basingstoke, Hampshire RG21 6XS and
175 Fifth Avenue, New York, N.Y. 10010
Companies and representatives throughout the world

PALGRAVE is the new global academic imprint of St. Martin's Press LLC
Scholarly and Reference Division and Palgrave Publishers Ltd (formerly
Macmillan Press Ltd).

ISBN 0–333–61078–4 hardback
ISBN 0–333–61079–2 paperback

This book is printed on paper suitable for recycling and
made from fully managed and sustained forest sources.

A catalogue record for this book is available
from the British Library.

Library of Congress Cataloging-in-Publication Data
Fleming, Peter, 1958-
      Family and household in medieval England / Peter Fleming.
         p. cm. – (Social history in perspective)
      Includes bibliographical references and index.
         ISBN 0-333-61078-4 – ISBN 0-333-61079-2 (pbk.)
         1. Family–England–History–To 1500. 2. Households–England–
History–To 1500. 3. England–Social life and customs– 1066–1485. I. Title.
II. Series.
HQ615 .F64 2000
306.85´0942--dc21

00-059127

10   9   8   7   6   5   4   3   2   1
10   09   08   07   06   05   04   03   02   01

Copy edited and typeset in *New Baskerville* by Password, UK
Printed in China

CONTENTS

This book is dedicated to my family
and to the memory of my father

ACKNOWLEDGEMENTS

I would like to thank Professor Ralph Griffiths for encouraging my early interest in the medieval family, and for his help and example ever since. Keith Dockray has given me the benefit of his wit, wisdom and enthusiasm in generous measure during the writing of this book, and to my wife, Ann Rippin, goes my deepest gratitude for having suffered its overlong gestation with patience and understanding.

INTRODUCTION

The family continues to be a favourite debating point among politicians and pundits. Today, we are frequently told that the 'traditional' family and family values are under threat, implying that these are to some degree 'natural', and have always been basically the same. Neither view is correct. Looking beyond modern European – and Europeanized – societies reveals that there is nothing essentially 'natural' about the defining features of the contemporary western family. Past and present societies outside the Christian European tradition have not always regarded unions based on the conjugal unit of husband and wife, monogamy, the aspiration, at least, to romantic love, or heterosexuality as constituting the sole acceptable framework for sexual relations, reproduction and the rearing of children.[1] Nor has the family stayed the same within European history. For one thing, there has never been one family type across the whole of Europe. Even within England, while it is now generally accepted that the 'nuclear' family of husband, wife and children was characteristic of society at least as far back as the fourteenth century, and probably beyond, the character of the English family has always been changing in a complex relationship with a host of factors touching virtually every aspect of life: political, legal, economic, social, cultural, religious, and even technological. The family, then, has a history.

That the changing nature of the English family can only be explained in relation to a wide diversity of factors demonstrates its historical centrality. This has been a reciprocal, dynamic relationship: as well as having been moulded by them, the family in its turn has been a crucial influence on each of these areas of human history. Over much of the English past, politics has been dynastic, to the extent that inherited power and the use of marriage as a political tool have been among its central characteristics. Many of the most important developments in English law have been prompted by the elites' desire to strengthen the family as a means for the orderly transmission of property down the generations. In addition to providing the most important framework for property ownership (at a time when the Church and the Crown were the only large corporate property owners – and, in any case, the latter is an extension of the royal family), the family is also the means by which succeeding generations of the labour force have been reproduced, so trends in family size and inheritance patterns have had a crucial impact on the distribution of capital and labour. The family is the primary forum in which children are reared – or 'socialized' – so that they may fit into adult society without too much disruption, and family relationships have played the major part in structuring society and determining cultural expectations. Finally, the demands of the family and household have encouraged technological developments, from house design to consumer goods.

Despite the family's centrality, there is no unambiguous, generally accepted usage of the word itself. 'Family' may be used today to indicate all the relatives of a particular individual, those relatives who live together under the same roof, the conjugal unit of married partners and their children, or even the children alone. The common thread is kinship: the relationship created by blood or marriage. 'Household' has a more settled meaning as: all those who usually live together under one roof, whether they are related or not. In classical and medieval Latin, *familia* denotes primarily a co-resident community – in other words, a household or the members of that household, including not only kin, but also servants – and in medieval England the distinction between family and household, in the modern sense, was usually absent. This should alert us to the probability that medieval people did not regard either family or household in modern terms, but it also means that, in order to discuss these topics in their medieval context, we need to assign them labels which were not actually in use at the time, and such a procedure is always problematic.

In this book I have adopted Lawrence Stone's definitions of 'family', 'household' and 'kin' as, respectively, 'those members of the same kin who live together under one roof', 'persons living together under the same roof' and 'persons related by blood or marriage'. In addition, the word 'lineage' is used to describe the entire kin group in its temporal dimension, including those dead, living or yet to be born.[2]

   This book concentrates on 500 years of the English family. While
there is some consideration of earlier developments, the real starting
point is the mid-eleventh century. This is not because I think that
the English Middle Ages in any sense 'began' in 1066, but not only
did the Conquest bring about a transformation in England's
political, legal and administrative systems, and many of these
changes had their impact on the family; it also pushed the evolution
of the family itself in a new direction. In addition, both the secular
and ecclesiastical law concerning marriage and inheritance took on
a new coherence and comprehensiveness in the two centuries
following the Conquest, and in this period the foundation was laid
for the legal framework of the family that would survive into modern
times.[3] Arriving at a terminal date for this study is more difficult,
but I would argue that the religious, administrative and ideological
changes brought about by the Reformation make the 1520s a suitable
decade in which to locate 'the end' of medieval England. The central
event between 1066 and 1530 occurred in the fourteenth century.
This was the demographic catastrophe, presaged by famine and fully
realized by plague, which in 1348–9 slashed England's population
by as much as 40 per cent. This plague, the 'Black Death', was a
watershed not only in England's demographic history, but also in
its social and economic development, and many historians argue
that this catastrophe brought about a major change in later medieval
family relations and structures. Further epidemics followed, and
England's population did not begin to recover until the early
sixteenth century.[4] Sustained population growth from the 1520s
provides another marker on the boundary between 'medieval' and
'early modern'.

   Attempting to cover five centuries of the history of the English
family and household in a relatively short space has meant that many
important issues have had to be only briefly sketched or largely
excluded. In particular, much more could be said about the
household as an economic unit, its physical environment, education,
and the wider political significance of the family. In addition,
comparisons have had to be kept to a minimum: this is very much a
study of the *English* family and household. To some extent, this
restricted focus can be justified beyond pleading lack of space. While
western Europe has long-standing common characteristics, each of
its constituent nations have their own peculiarities. Medieval

England had much in common with France, or with its neighbours within the British Isles, but it was also, like each of them, unique. Historians of medieval English society are blessed with an unusually rich body of evidence to work from, compared to most other areas of Europe in this period. As I hope will become clear, the amount of work which has been done on the English experience has left relatively few gaps needing to be filled by speculations based on foreign examples.[5] On the same principle, while the nature of medieval families varied greatly according to place, time and class, among other things, it is perhaps unwise to extend generalization and speculation much further through recourse to early modern examples: just as the life of a peasant family in 1100 was very different from that of their descendants in 1400, so we cannot assume that what can be demonstrated for the eighteenth century is also characteristic of the fourteenth.[6]

The family as a nexus of cultural practices and attitudes, as an institution created through laws and customs, as an economic unit, and as an ideological concept, is ever-changing, and so one cannot say that the modern family was ever 'created' at any particular point in history. However, it can be argued that the family as we know it today, in many of its most important external attributes at least, owes more to the centuries covered in this book than to any other period. This is particularly the case in the evolution of the process of marriage, and in the establishment of agreed laws of inheritance, but much of the ideology of the family – concerning the importance of consent and affection, for example – also received its definitive expression in this period. Therefore, the history of the English family in these five centuries, as well as being fascinating and important in its own right, also provides the key to understanding what came after.

Notes on Conventions

A Note on Money

The main currency units of medieval England were as follows:
One pound (£) = 20 shillings (20s.)
One mark = 13 shillings and four pence (13s. 4d.)
One shilling (1s.) = 12 pence (12d.)

Terminology

The Middle Ages are commonly divided into three sub-periods: 'early', ending in the eleventh century; 'central' or 'high', extending from the eleventh to the thirteenth centuries; and 'later', from the thirteenth to the fifteenth or early sixteenth centuries.

For the sake of simplicity, in this book 'villein' is used to denote the unfree, for whom there existed a number of different names depending on period, place and gradations in status.

Quotations

All quotations from primary sources have been translated into modern English.

1

MARRIAGE MAKING

Marriage in Theory and Law

Medieval conceptions of marriage derived from three sources. The first of these was imperial Rome, whose law code became a major influence on medieval jurists, both lay and ecclesiastical. The later Roman Empire also provided the means by which the second body of influences, the Judaeo-Christian scriptures and the writings of the early fathers of the Church, could be transmitted to the Middle Ages. Finally, the customs of the Germanic barbarians provided the foundation on which the components of Roman law and Judaeo-Christian teaching could be assembled into a new and resilient conceptual structure, most of which is still with us today.

Some of what the later Roman Empire understood as marriage would have been familiar in the Middle Ages. Marriage was monogamous. The minimum age at which marriage could take place was 14 for boys and 12 for girls, and both parties had to give their free consent to the union. The wife brought a dowry to her husband, but unlike medieval practice, he had to account for his use of it and, in the event of the marriage's dissolution, she could claim it back in its entirety. Far more alien to the later Christian law of marriage, divorce could be had with relative ease at the instigation of either husband or wife.[1] Medieval and Roman attitudes also parted company over the question of sex. Generally speaking, Greek and Roman culture was relaxed on the subject, although the increasing influence of Stoic philosophy and Gnostic beliefs in the late Empire encouraged many of the elite to distrust sexual pleasure. But even the Stoics did not regard sex as evil in itself, merely something that had to be kept within certain bounds.

While moralists might teach that the sole purpose of marriage was the procreation of children, there was a growing body of opinion that valued love and companionship between husband and wife.[2]

A very different attitude is apparent among the early Christians.[3] The Judaic tradition held that the sexual act polluted those who engaged in it, making ritual purification necessary before participating in sacred rites, but it did make a virtue of fecundity, and was at ease with the thought that husband and wife might actually enjoy sexual intercourse. During its development from a Jewish sect to a religion in its own right, Christianity retained the Hebraic notion of sex as pollutant, and in addition absorbed the Stoics' and Gnostics' suspicion of sensual pleasure. Some of the Church fathers built these beliefs into an asceticism that verged on the condemnation of all sexual activity as sinful. Such a view threatened the very idea that marriage (as a formal relationship between male and female sexual partners) could be compatible with salvation, a position that represented a radical break with classical and Judaic culture.

The Old Testament presented ample evidence of Hebrew marriage customs, but some of these, such as polygyny (Solomon was reputed to have had 700 wives), were plainly unacceptable to the consensus of opinion in the late Empire. However, the union of Adam and Eve gave a clear affirmation of monogamous marriage: 'Accordingly a man forsakes his father and his mother and adheres to his wife, and they shall be two in one flesh.'[4] This text is quoted with approval by Christ, who also taught that marriage was indissoluble by divorce, but despite this and his presence and miracle-working at the wedding at Cana, Christ's few recorded pronouncements on the family suggest an opposition between discipleship and traditional family relations.[5] In Matthew Christ declares: 'Truly, I have come to separate a man from his father, a daughter from her mother, and a daughter-in-law from her mother-in-law; and a man shall find his enemies within his own household. He who loves his father or mother more than me is not worthy of me, and he who loves his son or daughter above me is not worthy of me.'[6]

Paul's teaching is more amenable, if still falling short of a wholehearted commendation of marriage and family life. Paul saw marriage as a legitimate means of relieving sexual desire, for which purpose husband and wife should render to each other the 'marital debt':

But to avoid fornication, every man should have his wife and every woman should have her husband. The husband should pay the [conjugal] debt to his wife, and likewise the wife to her husband. The wife does not have power over her own body, but the husband does; and likewise indeed the husband does not have power over his own body, but the wife does. Do not refuse one another except by agreement for a period, to give time for prayer, and return to each other again so Satan does not tempt you on account of your incontinence.

However, he also saw marriage as inferior to his own state of celibacy: 'I wish that all could be as I am, but everyone has his particular gift from God, some of one kind, others of another, truly. Moreover, I say to the unmarried and widows: it is good for them if they remain as I am; but if they cannot control themselves they should marry: better to marry than to burn.' More positive is the correspondence he claims between marriage and Christ's relationship with the Church: Christ is to his church what the husband is to his wife; just as Christ loves the faithful, and they in their turn must obey him, so must the husband cherish his wife and she must obey her husband.[7]

Paul's doctrine on the family does allow marriage and the procreation of children a place in the scheme of salvation, and while he expects the wife to be subservient to her husband, his instructions to the latter to 'love his wife as himself' places him on the 'liberal' wing of early Christian opinion. However, the Pauline doctrine of marriage was not embraced by some of the early Christian writers who came after him. Their deep-rooted distrust of sex led them to believe that even sex within marriage was in varying degrees sinful. Established Christian opinion until the Reformation was agreed that virginity was the purest state; if one's virginity had been lost, then celibacy was second best, conceived of either as agreed sexual abstinence between married partners or, more usually, as a state maintained when one was free of the bonds of marriage; a sexually active marriage came a definite third.

The question of how, if at all, the sexually active married couple could avoid sin was where Pauline and more extreme Christian opinion parted company. The most prominent among this latter group was St Jerome. 'I praise weddings', he wrote, 'I praise marriages, but because for me they produce virgins'.[8] Jerome's debt to the Stoics is clear in his declaration that the man who loves his wife too much is guilty of adultery, a direct quotation from the second-century Stoic, Sextus (and repeated as recently as 1980 by Pope John-Paul II).[9] Jerome's position came close to asserting that, since sex was the expression of carnality and hence inherently evil, the procreation of children within marriage was incompatible with salvation.

Against this opinion stood St Augustine, the most influential of the church fathers. Augustine proposed that from Christian marriage flowed three positive results, or 'goods'. The three goods of marriage are offspring, fidelity and 'sacrament', or inseparability:

> In fidelity the focus is on the exclusion of intercourse with another woman or man outside the marriage bond. In offspring the focus is on loving reception, kind nurture, and religious upbringing. In the sacrament the focus is on the inseparability of marriage, and [on the requirement] that a man or woman, if dismissed, does not join with another for the sake of offspring. This is the rule of marriage by which the fruitfulness of nature is crowned, or the depravity of incontinence is regulated.[10]

This formulation provided the bedrock for most medieval discussions of Christian marriage. In contrast to Jerome's emphasis on virginity, Augustine welcomes fruitfulness within a Christian family. He also sees marriage as having an important social function in binding together families, thereby increasing harmony within the Christian community.[11] Nevertheless, Augustine does not eschew the notion that marriage is a remedy for lust, a safety valve whereby extramarital fornication may be avoided. The superiority of total sexual abstinence remains unchallenged.

The Germanic barbarians had institutions of marriage that were not wholly alien to late Roman practice. Formal marriage involved three stages: betrothal, the settlement of property, and the delivery of the bride from her father's authority to her husband's. The Germans practised a system of 'reverse dowry', whereby the bride – or her family – received property from the groom's family, with only a token offering given to the groom. The bride also received a 'morning gift' after her wedding night. However, the Germans also practised polygyny: the Merovingian King Dagobert was reported to have had numerous wives and concubines, 'like Solomon'. Husbands could readily divorce their wives, but wives could not divorce their husbands. Another Germanic custom frowned upon by the Church was the informal marriage, which did not involve the transfer of property or of authority over the bride, but required only the consent of bride and groom; such 'free' marriages were the ancestors of the clandestine unions which so troubled the medieval canon lawyers.[12]

While the Church never condemned the married state as incompatible with salvation, for centuries it was content to allow marriage to remain a largely civil affair, an arrangement made between the parties, regulated by secular authorities and contracted without the necessity of religious ceremony.[13] In England, the process whereby the Church developed its separate jurisdiction over marriage began with William I's edict of about 1072, designed to separate episcopal jurisdiction from that of the local secular courts, and reached its fulfilment in the Compromise of Avranches of 1172. During this 100 years the Church took over marriage jurisdiction from the Crown and other secular authorities, leaving the latter's competence in family matters largely restricted to questions of inheritance. The English experience was one of the earliest and most complete examples of a general phenomenon occurring throughout Christian Europe, whereby the Church assumed authority over marital questions.[14] Why did the Church want this jurisdiction, tainted as it was with carnality?

One answer is that the Church may have been reacting to what today might be called 'consumer demand': the laity increasingly wanted their unions blessed by the Church, and the necessity of deciding which unions were fit to be blessed inevitably dragged the Church into the regulation of marriage and family relations.[15] However, it was not drawn unwillingly into this area, but actively sought a greater role in the regulation of marriage. At this time the Church was fighting heretical movements whose common characteristic was the condemnation of the physical world, including human sexuality, as evil. As we have seen, there had long been a strong suspicion of all forms of sexual activity within orthodox Christianity, and this was a crucial factor in the Church's reluctance to involve itself with marriage, but now, in order to distance itself from the heretics' extreme views on carnality, the Church had to accommodate itself to marital sex. One consequence of this accommodation was the final acceptance, after much debate, of marriage as one of the Seven Sacraments. Its inclusion was controversial because it linked sex with the sacred, and it would be the only sacrament administered not by a priest, but by the laity: the bride and groom created the sacrament through their loving consent, following the example of Adam and Eve before the Fall.[16]

Perhaps, too, the Church's new-found interest in marriage was part of a campaign for the 'reformation of manners', an attempt to improve standards of behaviour and combat sin through closer surveillance and control of everyday life. This campaign was not just aimed at the laity; during this same period the Church was attempting to suppress clerical marriage or concubinage. Since at least the fifth century there had been a generally relaxed attitude towards clerical cohabitation with partners as man and wife, but from the early eleventh century the leaders of the Church insisted on clerical celibacy. By the beginning of the thirteenth century, prohibition of marriage for those who had taken religious vows was generally accepted and enforced, even if actual celibacy for all clergy remained an unattainable ideal. George Duby has argued that, once the mechanisms had been established for the suppression of clerical concubinage, the Church found it a relatively easy step to extend its jurisdiction over lay marriages. This process has also been seen as part of the so-called 'Investiture Contest', the Church's great struggle to free itself from secular lordship, symbolized in English history by the fatal conflict between Henry II and Thomas Becket. The advantages won by the Church in this contest drew it into the entanglements of the secular world to an unprecedented degree, but this time largely on its own terms, through its panoply of courts exercising canon law, combined with continuing involvement in secular government, administration and politics.

The growth of clerical jurisdiction over marriage is therefore an integral part of the general intrusion of ecclesiastical power into lay society in the twelfth century.[17] But this is not simply a story of the Church snatching power from resistant lay authorities. While emperors, kings and princes fought bitterly over other rights, in the case of marriage jurisdiction the demarcation lines were drawn largely by a process of agreement. Duby has described the process as it occurred in northern France as a struggle between an ecclesiastical and a lay aristocratic model of marriage, with the latter being gradually worn down by a process of attrition.[18] However, some doubt has been cast on this interpretation. David Herlihy has questioned the existence of a competing aristocratic model of marriage, suggesting that what Duby took as an alternative system was, in fact, nothing more than a series of departures from the clerical 'model', to which all members of the elite at least paid lip service, and there seems a greater likelihood that prelates and nobles – drawn largely from the same class, after all – worked together to extend ecclesiastical control over the recalcitrant lower orders, recognizing a common interest in the use of religion and canon law as a form of social control.[19]

Effective jurisdiction must be based on an accepted body of laws, and this had to be developed as the Church acquired its role as arbiter in marital disputes. One of the great achievements of the medieval Church was its formulation over a period of less than 200 years, and upon very sparse foundations, of a body of law and doctrine which is still deeply influential in western society. Before the twelfth century, the Church did not even have an agreed answer to the most basic question of what constitutes a valid marriage. Roman law and Germanic custom had long held the simple giving of consent between bride and groom as the essential act in the formation of a valid marriage, but this raised problems, since what could so easily be made might all too easily be denied or rescinded. In an effort to impose greater regularity over the couplings of the laity, the Church sought additional, or alternative, means of marking entry into a valid marriage. The main contender was the sexual act itself, combined with consent. However, Christians had a problem with this. Christ's mother had been a virgin at the time of his birth: Mary and Joseph had not, therefore, had sex. To accept sexual intercourse as a necessary constituent of a valid marriage meant that Jesus was the child of an unmarried mother, and this was obviously unacceptable. By the twelfth century, opinion had crystallized around the pronouncements of two contending theologians and canon lawyers, Gratian of Bologna, and Peter Lombard of Paris. Both accepted consent as a necessary precondition to a viable marriage, but whereas Peter Lombard saw consent alone as sufficient, Gratian believed that it had to be followed by sexual intercourse before a marriage could be created. Gratian lost the argument. After much discussion, Pope Alexander III (1159–81) adopted consent as the sole requirement for a valid marriage: the Church was forced to admit that it had no better answer to the problem than the Romans or Germanic barbarians, and resolved to live with the consequences. In England, this decision was promulgated in 1175 at the ecclesiastical Council of Westminster. Henceforth, marriage needed no more than the exchange of vows between man and woman; neither witnesses, priest, nor ceremony were required. There were two kinds of vows. By the exchange *per verba de presenti* the couple made themselves man and wife from the moment the words were spoken. Vows made *per verba de futuro* constituted a promise to marry at some point in the future. This promise was only binding if followed by sexual intercourse.[20]

The Church's adoption of consent as the sufficient constituent of a valid marriage has been regarded by Sheehan, among others, as a turning point in the history of western civilization, freeing individuals from the control of fathers and lords, and making a vital contribution towards the emergence of the modern companionate marriage. As such, it might be possible to see the Church's adoption of consent not only as an attack on the secular powers, but also as inviting social anarchy, with binding unions being entered into without any effective regulation. This was not the case. Far from being an ecclesiastical imperative, the principle of marriage made by consent was more a reluctant concession which, having been made, was as far as possible ignored in favour of the admonition to obey one's lords and elders. The degree to which real freedom of choice in marriage was available is the subject of much debate.[21]

The giving of consent could only create a valid union if the couple were free to marry. There were six major categories of impediment to marriage. Naturally, forced marriages were void, but the definition of force was restricted to violence, actual or threatened, which a court would judge to be more than a reasonably stable individual could withstand, a qualification subject to infinite interpretation, and peaceful cohabitation for any period was counted as consent. Pre-contract is another obvious impediment: people could not marry if already married to a living spouse. A second, bigamous, marriage was not always entered into knowingly. According to a suit brought before the London diocesan court, John Paynaminuta had not seen his first wife for 11 years, and believing her to be dead married a second time. Then someone told him that he had seen his first wife alive and well in Bayeux; reluctantly, John decided that he had no choice but to separate from his second wife, who consequently brought the suit against him. The evidence of one witness would not have stood up in court, and so as far as the Church was concerned the second marriage could continue, but John seems to have been convinced of his first wife's survival and felt himself bound by conscience to renounce his second wife. Pre-contract, real or pretended, could wreck an established marriage. In York, two marriages of 19 and 12 years' standing were brought to an end when the wife of one spouse was able to prove a 21-year-old prior contract with the other husband. The Church could only attempt to enforce unions that could be proven in court. What of the individual who could prove the existence only of a second, bigamous, marriage because the first had been contracted by the exchange of vows without witnesses? The church court would have to order the second marriage to be respected, if the first could not be proved, and by so doing order the couple to live in sin. In such a case, clerical opinion tended to recommend obeying one's conscience, and suffering the temporal consequences of disobeying the court, rather than imperilling one's soul.[22]

Parties to a marriage had to have reached the age of puberty, and in this the Church followed the Roman tradition, making valid marriage possible.for boys of 14 and girls as young as 12. Children who had been promised in marriage between the ages of seven and the age of puberty had to give their consent when they reached the latter age or else the union could not proceed. Children younger than seven could not be promised in marriage. However, there was an exception allowed where such underage unions were made in order to bring about or maintain peace, with the obvious application to marriages made between ruling families for diplomatic reasons.[23] The prohibition of clerical marriage provided another impediment.

Nor could a valid marriage be contracted by two people related to each other within the prohibited degrees of kinship. The basic dictum was that one could not marry a person from whom one might hope to inherit, but beyond this mercifully simple rule of thumb the precise rules were a far more involved matter. The medieval Church followed Roman practice in counting seven degrees of kinship within which a prohibited blood relationship was held to obtain. To find the degree of relationship between ego and a first cousin, for example, the Romans counted up from ego to ego's parent and grandparent, and then down through ego's uncle to the cousin, giving four degrees of relationship. However, the Germanic tribes had a different means of counting degrees, and it was this method which the Church adopted. The consequences were dramatic, for the Germans counted generations, not acts of generation. To return to the previous example: ego's grandparent is the common ancestor of ego and ego's first cousin, and the 'Germanic' counting of generations begins with the grandparent's children; the parents of ego and the cousin are the first generation, and ego and the cousin themselves the second, meaning that ego and the first cousin are related in the second degree. In short, counting this way approximately doubled the number of individuals caught within the seven-degree net of kinship. And that was not all, for to relatives by blood, or consanguinity, were added relatives by marriage, or affinity, relatives created by the exchange of an unfulfilled promise to marry in the future (the impediment of 'public honesty'), and also those with whom one had a spiritual relationship, drawing in godparents and their kin. This system was given papal authority by

Nicholas II's encyclical of 1059 and reaffirmed in England by an ecclesiastical council of 1075. In the words of Professor Brooke, 'the extreme rules of consanguinity established in the eleventh century were at once a marvellous excuse for cynics and a sad burden on tender consciences.'[24] The average medieval villager could have found few if any available marriage partners from within his or her own village if the system had been strictly operated.[25] Professor Sheehan has suggested that, by 1200 at least, English lay and clerical opinion treated four degrees of kinship as the limit within which unions were incestuous. In any case, the seven-degree rule was not to last, and the Fourth Lateran Council of 1215 bowed to the inevitable and instituted four degrees as the limit of impediment by kinship.[26]

Even at four degrees, the net of kinship was spread wide, and provided a powerful inducement to marital exogamy, that is, to marriage beyond one's neighbourhood or, perhaps, socioeconomic rank. St Augustine would have approved, for he taught that one of the justifications for marriage was that by creating alliances between different families, it strengthened the bonds within Christian society. Indeed, Professor Herlihy has suggested that by adopting such widespread prohibitions, the Church was applying Augustinian teaching to reduce the levels of inter-familial violence that obtained in early-medieval society. The prohibition on marriage within seven or four degrees forced heads of families to establish links with potential rivals and increased the circulation of women between families, thereby reducing the incidence of abduction and rape.[27] St Augustine certainly influenced popes and canon lawyers, but other reasons have been suggested for the adoption of such drastic kinship laws.[28] The cynical argue that the broad prohibition provided a lucrative scam for the Church and a convenient means of de facto divorce for the wealthy, since with so many potential marriage partners falling within the prohibited degrees, dispensations to marry a relative would have to be bought, while an inconvenient marriage could readily be annulled on grounds of consanguinity, affinity or spirituality.[29] Sheehan, for one, was inclined towards a more charitable interpretation; that the Church was merely trying to adapt scriptural precepts, in particular the ban on incest contained in Leviticus, to the contemporary situation, but the extent of the prohibition suggests an ulterior motive.[30]

The most audacious explanation has come from Jack Goody. For him, this prohibition needs to be seen alongside the Church's ban on divorce, polygyny and the adoption of heirs, as well as its championing

of consent, all measures, he believes, designed to restrict the incidence
of marriage and therefore the production of legitimate heirs, thereby
hampering the ability of propertied families to pass on their wealth.
The aim of this strategy was to divert property into the hands of the
Church, at a time in the eleventh and twelfth centuries when the clerical
estate was trying to assert itself against secular powers: lacking heirs,
testators would bequeath their property to the Church for the good of
their souls.[31] Goody's theory has proved controversial. There is no doubt
that many of the measures he identifies would have had some effect on
the production of heirs, but critics have countered that there is little,
if any, evidence of the clergy's desire or ability to engineer this result
and, in any case, the Church needed recruits from these same
propertied families, so the attempt to restrict legitimate procreation
would have been counterproductive. Goody's suggestion is also
vulnerable to the same criticism levelled at Duby's theory of contending
clerical and secular models of marriage, that such a fundamental and
sustained conflict between what are essentially two components of the
same elite class is highly unlikely.[32]

The Church held that marriage was instituted for the procreation of
children, and so impotence or infertility was another impediment. This
condition was often difficult to confirm with certainty. Couples had to
wait for three years before a claim of impotency could be tested. For
women, the test involved a physical examination to determine if the
hymen had been broken, thereby helping to establish if procreation
had been attempted. For men the examination was rather more
involved. In the dioceses of York, Canterbury, and probably Ely, a group
of seven 'honest women' was given this task. In York in 1433 one of
these women gave the court a detailed description of the examination:

> The same witness exposed her naked breasts, and with her hands warmed at
> the said fire, she held and rubbed the penis and testicles of the said John.
> And she embraced and frequently kissed the same John, and stirred him up
> in so far as she could to show his virility and potency, admonishing him that
> for shame he should then and there prove and render himself a man. And
> she says, examined and diligently questioned, that the whole time afore-
> said, the said penis was scarcely three inches long ... remaining without any
> increase or decrease.

The seven women then 'in one voice cursed him for presuming to marry
any young woman, deluding her that he could well deserve and please

her.'[33] The problems involved in proving impotence could lead to some embarrassing situations, and not only for the individual under inspection. A fourteenth-century case from the Ely episcopal register illustrates how the ecclesiastical court could find itself tied up in knots. After the marriage of John and Joan Poynant was annulled because of John's impotence Joan married another, and John managed to impregnate a woman whom he claimed to have been related to Joan's new husband. John, therefore, was not impotent after all, so his marriage with Joan was not void, but he claimed that his subsequent sexual adventure created a bar to the renewal of their marriage since it put the couple within the prohibited degrees of affinity through his lover's kinship with Joan's 'husband'; after two years, the bishop's court reached the decision that John and Joan should resume their marriage, irrespective of John's objection.[34]

There were other impediments, less frequently encountered. There were impediments of error – marrying the wrong person or marrying a villein in the belief that he or she was free – and the impediment of disparity of religion: marrying a heretic or nonbeliever. An adulterer could not marry his lover after his wife's death if he and his lover had known that he had been married and if they had either planned his wife's death or had planned to marry each other after her demise. While some of these categories suggest circumstances worthy of Jacobean domestic tragedy, the last might occur in cases where a couple entered into a marriage knowing – or subsequently discovering – a pre-contract, and the wife of the pre-contracted marriage died: if enforced, this rule would have prevented the couple from putting their union on a legitimate basis, and it seems that in such cases it was simply ignored.[35]

By the end of the twelfth century the canon law on marriage was comprehensive and sophisticated, probably more so than for any other subject within the Church's jurisdiction. In the realm of the Anglo-Norman kings matrimonial canon law was more systematically explicated and applied than anywhere else in western Christendom. The most intimate affairs of the laity were regularly scrutinized and judged by a clerical elite for whom direct experience of family life was supposed to be confined to memory and observation. The priest, as judge and confessor, now claimed to be the expert in marital relations. And yet the shadow of St Jerome, the urge to asceticism, still caused disquiet.

Throughout the Middle Ages, sainthood and family life were often portrayed as being at loggerheads.[36] The most influential theologian of the later Middle Ages, St Thomas Aquinas, had to battle against his mother and brothers in order to join the Dominicans. They imprisoned him for two years, and sent a 'lusty girl' to tempt him down the primrose path – all to no avail, of course. St Bernard of Clairvaux's decision to take holy orders was likewise opposed by his brothers. The father of St Francis of Assisi tried to imprison his son to prevent him from adopting a life of holy poverty, but the young saint 'flew naked to the Lord and put on a hair shirt'.[37]

However, there were notable exceptions to this pattern, such as St Elizabeth of Hungary. She was 'compelled to enter the state of marriage in obedience to her father's order', but none the less: 'She consented to conjugal intercourse, not out of libidinous desire but out of respect for her father's command, and in order to procreate and raise children for the service of God.'[38] Her motivation was therefore very much in line with the Augustinian justification of marriage. There were also instances of saints contracting 'mystical marriages'. One of the most notable is that of the thirteenth-century St Hermann of Steinfeld, in whose visions Mary appeared as his wife.[39] The cult of the Virgin Mary as mother, which flourished from the central Middle Ages onwards, also supplied a powerful affirmation of the value of family life.[40] In the fifteenth century the cult of Mary the mother was joined by that of Joseph the husband, although he could not, of course, supply the exact symmetry of fatherhood, at least with regard to Jesus.[41]

The theory of marriage and notions of ideal family life held by the Church were not necessarily shared by the overwhelming majority of the laity. Duby's hypothesis of two antipathetic views of marriage existing in feudal France, one ecclesiastical and one aristocratic, has already been noticed. Whatever the merits of this model in an English context, there is little doubt that the medieval laity could think for themselves about marriage and family relations. Beneath the visible edifice of Church teaching and judgement, there existed a substratum of tradition, custom and individual practice that was not systematically recorded, and whose existence has to be inferred from a myriad of disparate scraps of evidence. These notions are revealed through their realization in action, often in conflict with the ecclesiastical authorities.

Age at First Marriage

The average age at which first marriages are contracted is at the hub of an array of factors which are of central importance to the study both of the family and of the demographic profile of a given population. Age at first marriage may reflect the degree of control exercised over an individual's choice of partner since, by and large, the younger an individual, the less say they are likely to have in their marriage, because with age comes greater independence, both psychologically and materially. This in turn is likely to have an effect on the quality of married life, since partners who choose each other, and between whom there is no great disparity of age, are perhaps more likely to have a companionate marriage. Age at first marriage is partly determined by economic opportunities, assuming that couples tend only to marry if they are reasonably assured of their ability to support children. Thus the timing of marriage in medieval England was influenced by customary arrangements for the transmission of family assets from one generation to the next: were couples normally given a share of the family property, allowing them to set up independent households before the parents' death, or were they expected to live within a parental household, or did they have to wait until the parents' death or retirement before receiving enough property to allow them to set up a household, and how did these practices vary between elder and younger sons, sons and daughters, between urban and rural communities, and between rich and poor? Age at first marriage influenced the length of time heirs had to wait before inheriting, since the later the marriage, and hence the birth of children, in a couple's lifetime, the earlier their deaths will occur relative to their children's life-cycles. Finally, it has a crucial part to play in determining the demographic profile of a given community, since late marriage reduces the period within which the couple can produce children, and is therefore likely to place a brake on population growth.

In 1965 John Hajnal suggested that from the sixteenth century, north-west Europe conformed to what he termed the 'European marriage pattern'. This has three defining features: late age at first marriage (typically no younger than 26 for males, 23 for females), a small difference in ages between bride and groom, producing a 'companion-ate marriage', and a relatively large number of individuals (around 10 per cent) who never marry at all. Using studies of poll tax returns, some manorial court material, and the life-cycles of the well-documented higher nobility, Hajnal concluded that medieval English society at all levels was characterized by a high incidence of early marriage, including child marriages, and that there was a broad balance between males and females allowing the potential for almost universal marriage among the laity.[42]

Hajnal's pioneering work had to rely on a relatively small number of studies and available sources. Since its appearance a great deal more work has been done on the sources he used, new sources have been found, and new methods of analysis have been developed. Inevitably, his model has not escaped unscathed. Some of the most important contributions to the debate have been made by Richard M. Smith. Revisiting the 1377 and 1381 poll tax evidence, and supplementing this with the analysis of further manorial court records and comparison with continental European studies and sixteenth-century evidence, Smith has concluded that Hajnal's 'European marriage pattern' is characteristic of most levels of English society from at least the 1370s.[43] His conclusions are borne out by detailed studies of particular later-medieval communities such as the Lincolnshire manors of Spalding Priory, the manor of Kibworth Harcourt, Coltishall in Norfolk, the parishes of central and north Essex, York and Yorkshire, and Coventry, which all show at least one of the characteristics of late and companionate marriage and relatively large numbers who never married.[44] In addition, a large sample of wills from the period 1430–80 shows that 24.2 per cent of male testators died unmarried.[45] There are two exceptions to this general picture. One is provided by the work of Zvi Razi on the manor of Halesowen in Worcestershire from the thirteenth to the fifteenth century; the other arises from a consideration of elite marriage patterns. Both appear to show low ages at first marriage, consonant with a 'non-European' marriage pattern.

Razi's analysis is based on the reconstitution of tenant families, made possible by the unusually good survival of the Halesowen court rolls. From this genealogical data, Razi argued that his families' average age of first marriage was in the early twenties before the Black Death, and dropped to the late teens after it, with a high incidence of marriage, putting the Halesowen community into Hajnal's 'non-European' category.[46] This claim has been criticized by Jeremy Goldberg, among others. Goldberg's objections are based on what he claims to be a number of crucial assumptions made by Razi which cannot be substantiated from the manorial court evidence. Among these is the presumed link between inheritance, marriage and parenthood, namely that sons tended to enter their inheritance at the minimum legal age of 20, married at about the same time, and had their first child within a year. In addition, since the court rolls under-record those with little or no property, statistical models derived from them cannot be assumed to apply to the entire population of the manor.[47] Razi was actually aware of most of these methodological problems, and an element of educated guesswork is necessary in any attempt to model medieval populations and family structures. While Razi has since defended other aspects of his interpretation of the Halesowen evidence, criticisms of his treatment of age at first marriage do render Halesowen's exceptional character debatable.[48]

The second exception is perhaps more significant. Examples of early marriage among the gentry and nobility are not difficult to find. Mary, daughter and co-heiress of Humphrey de Bohun, Earl of Hereford, was married to Henry of Lancaster in 1380/1 when she was 11 years old at the most.[49] Richard, first-born son of Richard, Earl of Salisbury (d. 1460), who grew up to be Warwick the Kingmaker, was married at the age of eight; his two eldest sisters were also married as children.[50] Anne, the daughter and sole heiress of Sir Thomas Cobham of Sterborough in Surrey, was married to Edward Blount, second Lord Mountjoy, less than six months before his death in 1475 at the age of eight. Early marriage may have been something of a tradition in the Cobham family, for Lady Joan Cobham was first widowed in 1391 when she was but 12 years old. Her first husband, Robert Hemenhale, had apparently been knighted, and so there must have been a considerable disparity in their ages. A similar tradition of early marriage is evident in the fifteenth-century Plumptons, a gentry family of Yorkshire. Sir William Plumpton was married at the age of 12. He married his teenage son Robert to the six-year-old Elizabeth Clifford, and after Robert's death about four years later, a clause in the marriage contract came into force whereby Elizabeth would marry Sir William's younger son, William. The two infant daughters of this marriage Sir William promised in marriage after the death of their father in 1461. Examples of early marriage can also be found among the fifteenth-century Derbyshire gentry.[51] Canon law prohibited child marriage unless contracted as a means of peacemaking: this exception seems to have been interpreted with the utmost latitude in these and similar cases. Waiting until the parties were of canonical age could have its dangers. About 1154, Henry, Earl of Essex agreed with Geoffrey de Vere that his three-year-old daughter, Alice, should marry Geoffrey when she was 12, and delivered her to his care. This delay proved fatal to their plans, for after her twelfth birthday Alice contracted a clandestine marriage with Geoffrey's middle-aged brother, Aubrey de Vere, Earl of Oxford.[52]

However, in the later Middle Ages at least, such early marriages were the exception, even among the elite. Among later medieval landed and urban elites, the average age at first marriage of the daughters was probably between 17 and 24; for male heirs apparent it was about 21, and for younger sons between 21 and 26.[53] The average age at first marriage for 49 knights and esquires who were members of parliament between 1386 and 1421 was 21.8.[54] A wider social cross-section made up of testators in fifteenth-century East Anglia probably married for the first time in their mid-twenties.[55] Taken together, these figures put propertied society on the borderline between Hajnal's 'European' and 'non-European' marriage patterns, but demonstrate conclusively that child marriages were not the norm.

Purely on the basis of family strategy, upper-rank parents should have tried to arrange matches for their daughters and eldest sons at the earliest possible opportunity. With the ever-present fear of early death hanging over them, it was wise to marry off the heir apparent quickly, thereby preventing control of his marriage from passing to the family's feudal lord in the event of his father dying before he had attained his majority, and increasing the likelihood that he would produce a son of his own and so preserve the family line for one further generation. Daughters who remained at home unmarried were a drain on resources and, in terms of family advancement, a wasting asset. The longer a daughter remained unmarried, the greater the likelihood of her being abducted, coerced or seduced into an unsuitable marriage.[56] It is likely that many abductions were in fact elopements, and even when not manifested in such extreme acts of disobedience, there was the danger that post-pubescent sons and daughters would follow the stirrings of their hearts rather than the guidance of their parents. As Sir John Oglander put it in the seventeenth century: 'Marry thy daughters betimes [early], lest they marry themselves.'[57] However, the fact that there were not more marriages of children and adolescents suggests that other factors were at play. Some parents may have held out until the ideal match came along. The expense of providing dowries may have forced others to leave some time between marrying off their daughters. There is even the possibility that personal inclination, if not full-blown love, was allowed its say.[58]

On the other hand, the marriage of younger sons was not a priority for most landed parents. Many younger sons did not marry until they were into their late twenties, and some remained single. The nobility and gentry display a different pattern of marriage from those below them, and this can largely be explained by their greater wealth. With so much more at stake, and perhaps with a greater sense of lineage, the landed elite are likely to have arranged marriages at an earlier stage in the life-cycle, and to have left less to chance and personal choice, when compared with their social inferiors.[59]

The correlation between wealth and age at first marriage can also be detected lower down the socioeconomic hierarchy. Among the parishioners of later medieval Essex, for example, the incidence of marriage varied according to occupation and wealth. Those employed on the land tended to marry at an earlier age and to have had a greater chance of marrying overall than those involved in crafts and trade.[60] Those for whom wage labour constituted their main or sole income tended to marry late or not at all. Frequent movement in search of work and a precarious economic condition made marriage difficult, while most of those labourers who did marry were probably able to do so only after many years' saving to provide the basics of family life. Many were in this situation. Poos has calculated that 50 per cent of the post-Black Death Essex population were either totally or partially dependent on earning a wage.[61] Apprentices and household servants were usually unmarried, and so the widespread employment of young people in these occupations until their early to mid-twenties tended to raise the average age of first marriage. Demand for female servants was probably higher in towns, leading to a slightly higher proportion of females to males in urban populations, and a marginally later age at first marriage for urban women than their rural counterparts, perhaps early to mid-twenties in towns and late teens to early twenties in the country.[62]

Coercion and Freedom of Choice

Accepting that most levels of society, in the later Middle Ages at least, conformed to Hajnal's 'European marriage pattern' increases the possibility that most couples had some say in the decision to marry and in the choice of partner. The Church attempted to maintain a balance between acknowledging freedom of consent and insisting on the right of parents and lords to have a say in the decision to marry. The Church's teaching on consent was widely understood, but not always appreciated. In fifteenth-century Essex one father, John Corney, disapproving of his daughter Joanna's intended, was alleged to have announced, 'I love not the law, I will not let them.' Johanna persisted for a while in the face of opposition, but by the second reading of the banns the pressure had proved too much for her, and 'Johanna renounced [them], as is commonly said in that parish, at the instance of her father.'[63]

Goldberg has proposed that urban couples had more freedom from parental and seigneurial supervision over their courtship and marriage than their country cousins. Children who had entered service or apprenticeship in urban households had exchanged parental control for the supervision of master and mistress; the latter, Goldberg suggests, had less incentive to determine their charges' marital futures, since for most servants and apprentices marriage only came after the end of their term of service, and so their choice of partner had few material consequences for their erstwhile employers. In the countryside the young had fewer opportunities for employment outside the parental household, and for many the influence of their lord was inescapable, so freedom of choice would tend to have been restricted. However, within this general pattern there were variations between different farming areas, between the free and unfree, between different tenurial and inheritance regimes, and there were changes over time. For example, employment opportunities for young women – and hence the chance to escape close parental supervision – may have been greater in pastoral than in arable regions.[64]

Peasant families were usually involved in their children's marriages from an early stage. Most couples seem to have thought carefully about the decision to marry, and only took the plunge after discussion with parents, relatives and friends, which meant that the process, from the opening moves of courtship to solemnization, usually extended over a long period. Poos suggests that in Essex this applied even where little or no property was involved.[65] For most, parents, relatives and neighbours provided essential support during the difficult business of negotiating the marriage settlement, planning – and paying for – the wedding and setting up home afterwards.[66]

For many villein families, payment of the merchet, the fine owed to the lord for marrying a daughter, was an element in the costs of marriage-making. Merchet could be paid by the bride's father, by the bride or groom, or by another party, and records of who paid the fine have been used to suggest the balance between parental control and children's independence. For example, on the estates of Ramsey Abbey in the fifteenth century, father and bride each paid in a third of the recorded merchets, with the bridegroom paying in a slightly smaller proportion, indicating, perhaps, a high degree of independence on the part of intending couples. Furthermore, over half of the merchet-paying brides bought general licences, allowing them to marry whomever and whenever they wished, and did so without apparent assistance from their family. Hanawalt interprets this evidence as indicating that these women were probably able to arrange their own marriages, and were able to do so because they had saved for this eventuality from their earnings as servants. However, these merchet payments are not likely to have been particularly burdensome in most cases – the typical range being between 3d. and 4s. – and so the extent to which their payment can be taken as proof of financial independence is debatable: in some cases, might the bride's payment of her merchet represent her contribution to the overall costs of her marriage, most of which were borne by her family?[67]

Peasant couples shared in the common expectation that their marriages would have parental blessing, but there were the inevitable clashes. A Yorkshire case from 1490 presents one rare instance of resistance to parental wishes. The news of Elena Couper's betrothal to a bitter enemy of her parents provoked this furious reaction from her mother, 'thou filth and harlot. Why, art thou handfast with John Wistow? When thy father knows he will ding thee and mischew thee.' When she was eventually confronted by her father – in the neutral territory of a friend's house, and only after her father had promised not to harm her – she would not relent: on her knees before him, she declared, 'Sir, that I have done I will perform if the law will suffer it for I will have him whosoever say nay to it. And I desire no more of your goods but your blessing.'[68] Significantly, even in the extremes of her defiance, Elena still sought her father's blessing, indicating how deeply ingrained was the desire for parental approval, however grudgingly given.

Most medieval families did not enjoy the responsibility of transmitting sizeable patrimonies to their posterity. In the vast majority of marriages, it has been argued, the alliances created with the in-laws' family were relatively insignificant to the parents of bride or groom.[69] In purely rational terms, it might be expected that those parents for whom their children's marital choices could have few consequences for the family's future prosperity (either because the family as a whole had no significant wealth or because the children in question were younger sons who were not entitled to a significant proportion of the patrimony) would be content to let them make their own choices. But people do not behave simply on the basis of such rational calculations, now or in the Middle Ages. Personal likes and dislikes, the feeling that 'he isn't good enough for our daughter', and other judgements not based directly on strategies for the preservation and enhancement of wealth, surely had their part to play then as now. Elena Couper's plight may well have resulted from just such personal antipathy between her father and her intended. In a culture which placed such weight on parental consent, the temptation to use threats and coercion may have been too much for some disapproving parents, particularly if the recalcitrant child depended on a share of their property for the marriage settlement or to establish a new home. In any case, it would be wrong to assume that peasant families did not develop strategies for maintaining and enlarging their holdings, even if these consisted of only a few acres. Children still had to be provided for, and provision made for old age.[70]

There is an important difference between parental pressure and coercion. The former was generally accepted; when it tipped over into the latter, grounds were created for the annulment of the marriage. While the records of church courts suggest that this was a rare occurrence, there are cases of daughters being threatened with serious violence, imprisonment, cursing, or the loss of their inheritance if they did not agree to their parents' choice. In one instance, a woman alleged that her family arrived at the wedding armed with staves; in their defence, they claimed that they were only carrying these because they had used them to pole-vault across ditches on the way to the ceremony.[71]

The lengths to which some gentry parents would go are graphically illustrated by three fifteenth-century examples involving the Paston family of Norfolk.[72] Elizabeth Paston was nineteen years old when her mother, Agnes, and her brother, John, offered her as a possible bride to Stephen Scrope, a widower of about 50, and suffering from some unspecified physical deformity; this despite the clause in her father's will requesting that she be married to someone of comparable age. Scrope was enthusiastic, but Elizabeth less so; her reticence, apparently, prompted not by his age and appearance, but by doubts over his expectations as heir to his stepfather, the niggardly Sir John Fastolf. Soon, Elizabeth set her face against Agnes and John's plans for her marriage; or, possibly, having reconciled herself to the proposal, would not agree when Agnes and John changed their minds and rejected Scrope. In any case, Agnes Paston's response to her daughter's disobedience was extreme. According to Elizabeth's cousin, Elizabeth Clere, Agnes had placed her daughter under close confinement, and 'she hath since Easter the most part been beaten once in the week or twice, and some times twice on a day, and her head broken in two or three places.' The shocked Elizabeth Clere urged that a new and mutually acceptable suitor be found without delay. The marriage did not take place. Nor did several other possible matches contemplated for Elizabeth Paston during the late 1440s and early 1450s. Finally, in 1458, the problem child found a suitable husband in the person of Robert Poynings, a Kentish esquire.

Just under a decade later, Elizabeth's niece, Margery, fell foul of her mother, Margaret, and brothers, by falling in love with Richard Calle, the Paston's land agent. The couple contracted a clandestine marriage by exchange of words of present consent. When the family heard of this they rushed to prevent any communication between the pair, and their separation may have lasted for over two years. Margery's brother John was adamant that the family would not be disparaged by such a shameful marriage with a mere servant. Of Richard Calle he said, 'he should never have my good will for to make my sister to sell candles and mustard in Framlingham.' However much the Pastons may have sought to conceal it, the fact remained that Margery and Richard claimed to have contracted a valid marriage, and so in 1469 the bishop of Norwich intervened to test this assertion, despite Margaret's best attempts to dissuade him. Margery appeared before him. According to Margaret's letter to her son, Sir John Paston, the bishop did his duty reluctantly. Before asking her what form of words she had used in her vow to Richard, he reminded her of

> how she was born, what kin and friends that she had, and should have more
> if she were ruled and guided after them: and if she did not, what rebuke,
> and shame, and loss it should be to her, if she were not guided by them, and
> cause of forsaking of her for any good, or help, or comfort that she should
> have of them.

The bishop gave her every opportunity to deny that she had spoken binding words of present consent. To no avail: 'she rehearsed what she had said, and said, if those words made it not sure, she said boldly that she would make that sure before she went hence, for she said she thought in her conscience she was bound, whatsoever the words were'; 'These lewd words', wrote Margaret, 'grieveth me and her grandam as much as all the remnant.' Next, the bishop interviewed Richard Calle, who confirmed that binding words had been spoken. In the face of such determination, the bishop was forced to rule that they were indeed married. Thereafter, Richard and Margery lived together as husband and wife. Margaret's reaction to her daughter's stand before the bishop was to order her servants to turn Margery away from her door. Margaret's account of this incident throws a good deal of light on elite attitudes towards the uneasy balance of freedom and control in the choice of spouse. The bishop, portrayed as sympathetic to the Pastons, took pains to remind Margery of what she would be sacrificing: his warning neatly encapsulates the network of family, friends and neighbours from whom those looking for a marriage partner were supposed to take advice, and whose support and protection would be sorely missed in later life. But ultimately, he had to respect the couple's right to choose. Having established beyond doubt that their marriage, while irregular, was still valid, he had no choice but to declare them husband and wife. Margaret, for all her vitriol, had to do the same. To Sir John's suggestion of forcing a 'divorce', her response was unequivocal: 'I charge you upon my blessing that ye do not, nor cause none other to do, that should offend God and your conscience, for if ye do, or cause for to be done, God will take vengeance thereupon, [and] ye should put yourself and others in great jeopardy.' For all their ruthlessness, for all the shame that they perceived this match to have brought them, and for all that they believed Calle to be the ruination of one of their own, the Pastons dared not break asunder those married in the sight of God. Richard Calle had known this, and offered it as a rare comfort in a letter he managed to smuggle to his wife during their enforced separation: 'four times in the year are they accursed that prevent matrimony ... God will of His rightwiseness help His servants that mean truly, and would live according to His laws.'[73]

Four years later a marriage was being negotiated between William Yelverton and Margery's sister Anne. But like her sister, Anne was too friendly with one of the Paston servants, John Pampyng, for her brothers' liking. Sir John warned his brother, 'I pray you beware that the old love of Pampyng renew not.' Determined not to have a virtual repeat of the sorry episode between Margery and Richard Calle, the Pastons dismissed Pampyng, and the marriage went ahead. These three cases show the strengths and limitations of consent. Once made, the vow of present consent had to be respected, but a ruthless family could make a nonsense of the doctrine of freedom of choice for all but the strongest and most determined of its members.

At both the highest and the lowest levels of medieval society, paternal influence was accompanied by feudal authority. The marriages of villeins required their lord's consent, at least in theory, while before the thirteenth century the daughters and widows of vassals had to have their lord's permission before marrying – again, theoretically if not always in practice. In addition, the lord enjoyed the right to arrange the marriage of his vassal's underage heir. These rules stemmed from the basic notion of feudal society that the lord should be able to choose who was to be his vassal or tenant. By her marriage, the heiress to a fee or tenement could deliver it into the possession of a vassal or tenant who was unacceptable to her lord, who was therefore justified in intervening in her choice of partner. In addition, a lord might need to prevent the marriages of his tenants' daughters to partners who lived outside his manor, since this could result in a loss of labour both in the person of the daughter and also, potentially, in her offspring. After the Angevin legal reforms of the thirteenth century, lords could no longer intervene in the marriages of their vassals, with the crucial exception of the king. He retained this right over his immediate vassals, and so tenants-in-chief continued to make their marriages with at least the possibility of royal intervention, although this was probably uncommon. Henry I (1100–35) had promised in his coronation charter that while his barons were obliged to consult him over the marriages of their female relatives, he would not exact any payment from them in return, and would only intervene if they proposed marriage to one of his enemies. Sidney Painter found no instances of twelfth-century kings prohibiting the marriages of their tenants-in-chief. However, early in the following century King John (1199–1216) seized the dower property of at least one widow after she had refused to marry as he had directed, and obtaining the right to remain single or marry as one wished continued to be an expensive business for many widows and heiresses.[74]

The marriages of villein daughters and widows remained subject to seigneurial regulation. Before the mid-thirteenth century, the Church generally supported the lord's right to control the marriages of his serfs, but thereafter the emphasis changed to stressing the validity of serf marriage whether the lord's consent had been obtained or not, and the new thinking on this matter was swiftly disseminated throughout western Christendom.[75] While later medieval church courts would not countenance blatant seigneurial coercion in villein marriages, lords were still left with potentially powerful means of influencing the marital choices of their unfree tenants. There has been much debate on the use lords made of merchet to determine unfree women's timing of marriage and choice of partner. In the 1970s Eleanor Searle argued that lords used merchet as a means of controlling peasant marriages in order to ensure that their new tenants were acceptable. This view has been challenged by Brand, Hyams and Faith. Brand and Hyams argue that after the thirteenth century at least, it was no longer acceptable for lords to intervene directly in their villein tenants' marital choices, and so merchet became nothing more than another tax on villein tenants, albeit one of the more irksome and resented, since its payment was regarded as the acid test of an individual's unfree status. Rosamond Faith agrees that merchet was not used coercively in later medieval manors, but sees its significance as being more symbolic than fiscal. Merchet, she argues, was levied even on poor cottagers in amounts so small as to have been hardly worth collecting if revenue was the point at issue, indicating that its function was to remind villein tenants of their servile status. While this may well have been a factor, and while lords would have had the ability to bully their tenants into or out of marriage if they had so wanted – not necessarily through the use of merchet – the majority of opinion tends to see merchet, in all but a few cases, as merely yet another feudal tax, levied according to the wealth of the bride or her family, and not used to manipulate marital choice.[76]

However, while the average merchet payment was relatively low, it could occasionally be manipulated to the point where disobedience was prohibitively expensive, or used quite simply as a punishment for some unrelated matter.[77] If lords did attempt to prevent their female tenants marrying outside the manor, their efforts were largely ineffective. For example, in the priory of Spalding's manors in the late thirteenth century fewer than half of the female villeins married within their manor. Similar patterns have been found in later medieval Cambridgeshire and on the bishop of Worcester's manors.[78]

Seigneurial influence could be exerted in other ways. Lords could be jealous of their right to be consulted on the marriages of their tenants. In one notorious case of about 1220, after one of his more prosperous tenants refused to consult with him about the marriage of his daughter, Henry de Vere broke into the man's house at night in search of the girl; her mother bundled her out of the window to escape from him, but he then broke into the family's barn and set it alight, either by accident or design.[79] Before the fourteenth century, villein widows were often instructed to marry by their lords so that their household would be more able to supply the required labour and services, and while it is unlikely that they were often told whom they should marry, there are instances of rather heavy-handed seigneurial direction.[80] In 1289 one Cambridgeshire villein widow paid a fine of one shilling to buy time while she found a husband of her choosing rather than her lord's.[81] While a lord might select a spouse for a woman on his manor, she was free to reject him on payment of a fine. In other cases, lords stepped in to take the place of a deceased father by arranging the orphaned daughter's marriage. A lord could refuse to accept the husband of a female tenant, thereby preventing him from taking on her holding.[82] Lords might also put pressure on their male servile tenants to marry. On a thirteenth-century Cambridgeshire manor Thomas Robynes preferred to pay a fine rather than marry Agatha of Hales as ordered, while another villein was distrained because he would neither pay a fine nor take a wife.[83]

Marriage Strategies

For the propertied classes, marriage was the prime means of advancing the interests of the family. A successful match could provide an alliance with a family which had influence with the king or the nobility, standing and power in the locality, social status, money and lands, and it was through marriage that the family name and patrimony were maintained. At this level, marriage could not be simply a matter of love.

For kings, marriages to wealthy heiresses sometimes provided the means of endowing their own families. Edward III, having handsomely endowed his eldest son, the Black Prince, with lands from the royal demesne, relied on marriage to provide for three of his remaining four sons: Lionel was married to Elizabeth, daughter and heiress of William, Earl of Ulster; John of Gaunt was married to Blanche, daughter and co-heiress of Henry de Grosmont, Duke of Lancaster; and Thomas of Woodstock was married to Eleanor, daughter and co-heiress of Humphrey de Bohun, Earl of Northampton, Hereford and Essex.[84] For Edward III, marriage solved the problem of how to provide for a large family. For Edward IV, the need to use marriage as a means of providing for a large family – acquired along with his wife, Elizabeth

Woodville – created problems. What seemed to contemporaries like the monopolization of the upper reaches of the marriage market by the King's Woodville in-laws after 1464 was an important factor in the alienation of the Earl of Warwick and Edward's own brother, the Duke of Clarence, with near fatal results for the Yorkist dynasty.[85]

As a means of enhancing family wealth and influence, marriage was a game of chance. The bride who brought only her dowry to a marriage could, by the right order of deaths among her relatives, turn overnight into a wealthy heiress; on the other hand, failure to produce an heir could result in an inheritance acquired through marriage being lost to the male line in the next generation. For Richard Neville, Earl of Warwick, the cards fell almost perfectly. His marriage in 1436 to Anne, daughter of Richard Beauchamp, Earl of Warwick, looked useful but, with Anne's father and brother still alive, hardly likely to propel Richard to the top of the magnate pile. The deaths of her father in 1439, her brother in 1446, and his daughter three years later, brought Richard the massive Beauchamp inheritance and with it, an earldom.[86]

Different strategies might be adopted depending on whether the child to be married was an eldest son, younger son or daughter. Eldest sons generally found brides of equal or higher rank than their own, while daughters and younger sons were usually married into families of lesser status. In this way, most noblemen had in-laws among the gentry, and marriage across the ranks made an important contribution to the cohesiveness of landed society. In most cases it accorded with sensible family strategy to marry off daughters: after the passing of the *maritagium* in land daughters need not carry with them parts of the family patrimony with their marriages, and the alliances thus made could prove useful. For younger sons it was a different matter since their brides would have a claim on a share of the family estates as jointure or dower. Consequently, the marriage of younger sons was not usually a priority, and this fact, combined with dubious prospects of inheriting much more than a fraction of their parents' wealth, left many of them facing an uncertain future.[87]

How was news of an available match disseminated? Family connections were probably the usual means, but contacts with business partners or with friends and colleagues in the law, in royal or civic office or within a lord's affinity might also play their part. For all the Church's restrictions on marriage with kith and kin, the convenience of repeated marriage between families with shared interests led many propertied families to create dense networks of relationship.[88] In the

Kent-Sussex Weald, the Guildfords married twice into the Pympe family of Nettlestead, near Maidstone, and three times into the Hautes of the Stour valley.[89] Merchants usually married the daughters or widows of other merchants with whom they did business. Such economic relationships were often accompanied by office-holding, and intermarriage within the urban governing class did much to enhance elite solidarities.[90] Business associates were also useful contacts within landed society. During the reign of Edward IV the Kentish gentleman Robert Brent married Joan, a widow, whose former father-in-law, John Crekyng, had numbered among his feoffees two of Robert's kinsmen, William and Roger Brent.[91] The Cinque Ports confederation in Kent, Sussex and Essex provides an example of how connections within local jurisdictions could provide marriage partners: by 1472 Thomas Hexstall, mayor of Dover, had married Jane, the widow, successively, of John Coppledike, a wealthy bailiff of Winchelsea, and of Richard Cook, mayor of Sandwich; all three towns were Cinque Ports.[92]

The legal profession could provide another pool of potential spouses. The intensity of intermarriage among early Tudor lawyers did much to strengthen their sense of themselves as a professional community. Two striking examples of professional endogamy are provided by the families of Catesby and Roper. Justice John Catesby (d. 1487) married the daughter of an Exchequer clerk; his son and grandson married lawyers' daughters and a granddaughter married first the son of a prothonotary and then a judge of Common Pleas. John Roper, Henry VIII's attorney, married the daughter of a chief justice; Roper's two daughters married a baron of the Exchequer and a chief justice, and his eldest son, William, married Margaret, daughter of Sir Thomas More, briefly Henry VIII's chancellor. Exchequer connections appear to have facilitated the marriages of William Page, a teller of the Exchequer by 1509: his first wife was the daughter of a fellow teller, and his second was the daughter of Sir Humphrey Starkey, chief baron of the Exchequer.[93]

The royal household provided another forum for matchmaking. A number of Richard II's household and retinue were related by marriage, such as king's knight Thomas Clanvowe, husband of a damsel of the Queen's chamber. The Haute family were related to Queen Elizabeth Woodville, and were familiar figures at the courts of Edward IV and Henry VII. They married into their fellow courtier families of Guildford, Fogge and Roos.[94] While there may often have been other factors bringing couples together, the number of relatives by marriage within the royal household is highly suggestive.[95]

For the propertied classes, London became increasingly important as a clearing house for the latest information on potential spouses. The Pastons of Norfolk certainly found their visits to the city useful in this regard. In 1478 John Paston wrote to his mother:

> I heard while I was in London where was a goodly young woman to marry, which was daughter to one Seff, a mercer, and she shall have £200 in money to her marriage, and 20 marks by year of land after the decease of a step mother of hers, which is upon 50 years of age; and ere I departed out of London, I spake with some of the maid's friends, and have gotten their good wills to have her married to my brother Edmund.[96]

The children of London merchants often provided suitable matches for gentry families. For the Londoners, marriage with a gentry family provided prestige and useful connections; for the gentry, it promised ready cash, a fact that prompted suspicions among some merchants that they were being milked by financially embarrassed gentlemen. While the nobility and the greater gentry might have considered a mercantile match below them, there were still plenty of interested fathers in the lower reaches of gentle society: in the fifteenth century, one-third of the wives of London aldermen came from landed families.[97]

Marriage negotiations among the propertied elites were on occasion businesslike to the point of callousness. In 1413 two Derbyshire gentry fathers drew up a marriage contract with a blank space where the bride's name should have been, since one of them had not yet decided which of his daughters he would marry off; another Derbyshire contract provided that the grandson of the one party would marry 'one of the daughters' of the other, suggesting that here too, the decision to ally the two families came first, and the personal feelings of the young people who would bring this about had hardly been considered.[98] On this evidence, one might suppose that the medieval gentry had never encountered Paul's injunction that the husband should 'love his wife as himself', but this may not have been the whole story.

In letters of the fifteenth-century gentry and merchants, protestations of love are surprisingly common amid the hardheaded discussions about the wealth and expectations of potential spouses. In his letters to his kinsman Sir Robert Plumpton, the lawyer Edward Plumpton praised the personal qualities of his intended bride, Agnes Drayate, a London widow, whom he described as 'goodly and beautiful, womanly and wise, as ever I knew any, none other dispraised: of good stock and worshipful

... She and I are agreed in our mind and all one', although a cynic might suspect that his fulsome words were in part designed to persuade Sir Robert to provide him with the additional 20 marks demanded for her jointure.[99] The Stonors legal advisor, Thomas Mull, neatly caught the balance between Cupid and Mammon in his question to William Stonor, the rather halfhearted wooer of Margery, the widow of a son of Lord Mountjoy:

> I would know this of you: and the case were so that she would be agreeable to have you with £40 or 80 marks jointure, would your heart then love as ye have done before this season? ... But one thing I dare say in my conceit, that she on her part since your departure hath been vexed and troubled with the throws of love more fervently in her mind than ye have been since vexed with her sayings ... I know once for certain she loved you as a perfect lover, and that right late never better than the last season that she was in London ... whereas she may revolve at her liberty without controlling every thing that longeth to love's dance, though the flame of the fire of love may not break out so that it may be seen, yet the heat of love in itself is never the less, but rather hotter in itself.

Thomas Mull sees Margery's love afflicting her like a fever, from which she desires relief, 'as the man in the water desireth to be relieved from drowning in the peril of the sea', and he promises to show William how he may use her predicament to drive a better bargain![100] Agnes Wydeslade, a wealthy, childless widow, was pursued, successfully, by Sir William Stonor, 'to whom her heart is set'.[101] In 1476 the wool merchant Thomas Betson was betrothed to Katherine Ryche, the daughter of Elizabeth Stonor. He wrote to her from Calais a love letter that often reads like the awkward solicitudes of a rather distant uncle for his teenage niece, which is hardly surprising, since Katherine was no more than fourteen at the time. He urges her to 'be a good eater of your meat always, that you might wax and grow fast to be a woman', but adds, in more conventional lover's terms, 'for when I remember your favour and your sad [serious] loving dealing to me wards, for sooth ye make even very glad and joyous in my heart.'[102]

The Pastons could be ruthless players in the marriage game, but not all members of the family lacked a softer side to their character. The love letters between John Paston III and Margery Brews are famous early examples of the genre. In February 1477, while tough negotiations went on between their families, Margery sent two Valentines to her lover and future husband:

> And if ye command me to keep me true wherever I go,
> Certainly I will do all my might you to love and never no more.
> And if my friends say, that I do amiss,
> They shall not me hinder so for to do,
> Mine heart me bids evermore to love you
> Truly over all earthly thing,
> And if they be never so wroth,
> I trust it shall be better in time coming.

But Margery shared with Thomas Mull an appreciation of the balance between sentiment and the economics of courtship: 'And I let you plainly understand that my father will no more money part withal in that behalf but £100 and 50 mark, which is right far from the accomplishment of your desire. Wherefore, if that ye could be content with that good, and my poor person, I would be the merriest maiden on Earth.'[103] These examples of sentiments exchanged between prospective spouses perhaps raise the suspicion that such expressions were to some degree convention, the expected accompaniments to the wheeling and dealing over dowry and jointure. Certainly, it is hard to imagine that love – as opposed to liking and the recognition of shared interests – often resulted from the brief and infrequent meetings that seem to have constituted courtship among many of the landed and mercantile classes.

Marriage Settlements

For families with any kind of property to their name, the simple words of consent between bride and groom were accompanied by negotiations concerning the lands, rents, money or goods to be exchanged. Those who were marrying for the first time – and thus young and under the control of their elders – had these negotiations conducted on their behalf by parents or guardians. Widows might also look to a male relative to negotiate their next marriage. Settling these matters could involve long and complex negotiations, as Chaucer remarked of the marriage settlement between a knight and his intended:

> I swear it were too long you to tarry,

If I you told of every script and bond,
By which that she was feoffed in his land[104]

Dowry and dower – in the later Middle Ages supplemented by jointure
– were the essential components of marriage settlements. The dowry –
also known as the portion – was given by the father of the bride to the
groom or his family, and was originally intended as a contribution
towards the upkeep of the bride. Until the mid-thirteenth century this
was generally land (*maritagium*), but thereafter it usually took the form
of a money payment. The change from land to cash may probably be
seen as a reflection of an increasingly commercialized society, where
the propertied classes were becoming more used to handling cash
transactions. Land given as dowry had the disadvantage that it would
be lost to the family of the bride.[105]

The value of dowries varied considerably according to several factors,
including the number of daughters for whom provision had to be made,
and the relative standing of the two families. Potential sons-in-law of
higher social status, political influence or greater wealth would
command larger dowries; where the balance of advantage tipped in
the daughter's favour less need be spent on enticement. In most cases,
parents had to provide for what might be a considerable item of
expenditure if their daughters were to find suitable matches. The
average dowry given by baronial families between 1300 and 1500 was
in excess of 100 marks. Dowries paid by fifteenth-century gentry usually
amounted to between five and 11 times the annual rental value of the
jointure promised to their daughters. In the fifteenth century a father
with 800 marks to spend on a dowry could realistically hope to catch a
son-in-law of knightly rank and a jointure worth £120 a year. But this
was a vast sum to find. Not surprisingly, the payment of such large
sums was usually made by instalments. From the late thirteenth century,
marriage settlements regularly provided for the repayment of part of
the dowry if the bride predeceased her husband without leaving
children by him, since this left him free to contract another marriage
with his 'market value' largely intact.

The second element in the father's provision for his daughter was
the trousseau, or chamber. This was usually jewels, clothes and other
personal belongings that the bride would take to her marriage, and
which, while used by her, would become the property of her husband,
since under common law all the bride's moveable goods, or chattels,
became the groom's property after their marriage. However

burdensome such payments were, the wise father was loath to leave any of his daughters unwed. Each unmarried daughter was a lost opportunity, a wasting asset if not used to tap into networks, to consolidate holdings, to play the biological lottery that might, one day, through circumstances unforeseen at the time of marriage, transform her family's fortunes through the windfall of a rich inheritance.[106]

The other major part of the marriage settlement was intended to safeguard the position of the wife in the event of her being widowed. Under common law, any freehold land the wife held in her own right remained hers, but was under her husband's control, to revert to her in the event of her widowhood. But a woman who was not an heiress might face widowhood without any means of supporting herself, unless she could claim dower. Dower, that part of her husband's property which a widow would receive for her support after his death, was already well established when the Normans came. Before the Conquest, bridegrooms or their families had to indicate what provision they had made for the bride's widowhood before the marriage could proceed. The Anglo-Saxon widow had a life interest in her dower property: she could neither dispose of it during her lifetime nor bequeath it at her death, for at this point it reverted to the heirs of her deceased husband.[107]

There were two main categories of dower recognized by common law: 'nominated' (*dos nominata*) and 'reasonable' (*dos rationabilis*).[108] Nominated dower was allocated to the bride at the time of her marriage – at church door – and consisted of a specified – nominated – share of the property which the groom held at that moment. The property with which the bride was endowed was usually made up of land – but could alternatively or in addition consist of rents, goods or money. The property nominated as dower could not exceed one-third of all the property of which her husband was seized at the time of allocation, but there was no legal minimum share. The woman could take possession of her nominated dower immediately after being widowed.

Reasonable dower was created by the common law's assertion that all widows of men who held lands of free tenure were entitled to a reasonable share of all the lands which their husbands had held at any time during the marriage, and even embracing land granted away without the widow's permission. For the military tenures of knight service and serjeanty, this reasonable share was judged to be a third; for widows of tenants by socage, the share was often a half. Until the thirteenth century, property acquired after the marriage was excluded from reasonable dower. This had obvious disadvantages for the widow if her husband's wealth increased significantly after their marriage, which it would do if he subsequently came into his inheritance. This problem was addressed by the 1217 revision of Magna Carta, which established that reasonable dower was henceforth to be assigned from all the property held at the time of the husband's death. With both nominated and reasonable dower the widow had only a life interest: on her death the dower property reverted back to her deceased husband's heirs.

Reasonable dower had superseded nominated dower at the latest by the beginning of the fourteenth century, and its triumph owed a good deal to lawyers' constructions of the clauses in Magna Carta concerning dower. A woman who accepted nominated dower at her marriage thereby barred her right to reasonable dower, and since nominated dower could amount to less than one-third of her husband's property, in some cases such acceptance would have been against her interests. This was particularly so after 1217, when, by accepting nominated dower, the bride could have been rejecting a greater share not only of her husband's existing property, but also of the much larger estate he might hold at his death. However, reasonable dower also had serious weaknesses from the widow's point of view. Apart from the difficulties of claiming dower from her husband's heirs, there were several ways in which the bride's expectation of a comfortable widowhood could be dashed. The husband's estates could be forfeited for treason – a not uncommon situation among the gentry and nobility in times of civil strife – he could predecease his father, and so never enter into his inheritance, or his father could disinherit him; in each case, his widow would have nothing from which to claim her dower.

The widow's interests faced an additional threat from a lawyer's stratagem that became practically ubiquitous among property holders during the later Middle Ages. For a variety of reasons, landholders often found it convenient to separate the common-law title to their land from the enjoyment of its profits and control over its disposition. They did this by means of the enfeoffment to use. An enfeoffment is a grant of land, a feoffor (or *cestui que use* in legal terminology) the person who grants it, and the feoffee the person to whom it is granted. The enfeoffment to use creates a trust, made up of a group of feoffees – trustees – who are granted the land on condition that the feoffor continues to enjoy the rents and other profits from that land, as well as control over its disposition. The trust is based on the legal fiction that the property rightly belongs to the feoffees, not to the feoffor. Common law did not allow the free disposition of land after death, which made it technically impossible to bequeath land by will. The use could circumvent this prohibition. By the 1290s at the latest, landholders were employing the use to give themselves the power to dispose of their lands after their deaths to whomsoever they wished. Enfeoffment to use could also be employed to convey land during the holder's lifetime (*inter vivos* transactions), to change the tenure of land, and to escape dues and services owed to the feudal lord. Until a statute of 1377 it provided a refuge for debtors against their creditors, and only after a 1398 statute were lands held to the use of a convicted traitor forfeitable.[109]

Crucially for the widow, however, the use could cheat her out of her dower. Property which had been enfeoffed to the use of a prospective groom before marriage could not be claimed as reasonable dower, since as far as common law was concerned, the feoffor no longer held it at the time of the marriage. Such an eventuality could easily be avoided if the bride's father took the basic precautions, but what if her father-in-law enfeoffed all his lands to his use before his son inherited? The feoffees might be instructed to continue to hold them to the son's use after his father's death, so that while the son enjoyed the profits, he did not actually have a common-law title to the land. In theory then, a man who had vast estates, all held to his use, could be regarded by the common law has having nothing from which his widow could claim her dower.

The answer to this predicament came in the form of the jointure. This was an agreement – made between the families of bride and groom at the time of the marriage – by which the couple were granted property by the father of the groom which was to be held by them in joint survivorship, so that if the wife were widowed, the jointure would be held solely by her for her lifetime. After her death it would revert to her husband's heirs. Even if the son predeceased his father, the son's widow would still be entitled to her jointure. Unlike reasonable dower, which the woman did not already hold at the moment of her widowhood and had to claim from her husband's heir, she held her jointure with her husband during his lifetime and at his death she automatically became sole seized of it, without the need to sue a writ of dower against the heir. And, from 1388, jointure, unlike dower, could not be legally forfeited for the husband's treason. Jointure, by the fact that the widow had only a life interest, had the advantage for the groom's family that land was prevented from passing out of the family permanently. While a second husband could not expect either himself or his heirs to inherit his wife's jointure lands, he could still enjoy the revenues which accrued from them while the marriage lasted. Hence, even widows whose main economic asset was only a jointure need not have had their attractiveness too badly tarnished in the eyes of prospective suitors.[110] Jointure became popular after 1285, when the Second Statute of Westminster's chapter *De donis conditionalibus* prevented a man from disposing of property he held by way of jointure.[111]

The various elements of a marriage settlement, dowry, trousseau, jointure and dower are present in the contract drawn up in 1429 between William Haute, an esquire in the Calais garrison and a widower, and Richard Woodville, lieutenant of Calais. By the terms of this document William agreed to marry Jane, Richard's daughter. He pledged lands to the annual value of £66 13s. 4d. as their jointure, and dower lands worth £40 per year, all to be chosen by Richard from among the Haute estates. For his part, Richard agreed to provide a dowry of £266 13s. 4d. to his prospective son-in-law, as well as his daughter's trousseau and jewels, and to meet the costs of the wedding. But there was a problem. Some of the property William had agreed to settle on Jane was not his to give, since he had previously entailed it on his daughter by his first wife. This daughter was his sole heiress, and herein lies the importance of the Woodville marriage to William's plans: he needed a son, or else his branch of the family would die out in the male line. The hapless girl could not perpetuate the family name, and so her interests had to be sacrificed. In the contract William agreed to disinherit her by whatever means he and Richard could devise, short of forcing her into a nunnery.[112]

But what of the case whereby a father disinherits his son, thereby leaving nothing from which the son's widow could claim dower? Such an eventuality might occur because the father remarries and provides the jointure for his second wife from property that had been earmarked for the son of his first marriage, or disinherits his first son in favour of a son by a second marriage. From at least the 1320s it was common for marriage settlements to include clauses preventing the father of the groom from harming his son's interests in this way. Such restrictive settlements grew more sophisticated as it was realized that the same device could be used to exempt certain properties from the eldest son's inheritance. For example, the father might wish to endow younger sons, or daughters, or to provide for religious benefactions.

Increasingly, such arrangements became part of the negotiations
leading to a marriage settlement since they directly affected the bride's
dower.[113]

By the end of the fifteenth century, such restricted settlements,
concerned with dower, had been joined by the entailed use, concerned
with jointure. This device was created by enfeoffing the property of
the groom's father to his use and to the use of certain of his heirs, for
example, his son and daughter-in-law, and after their deaths to the
legitimate heir of their bodies – their eldest son, or daughters for want
of surviving male offspring – and, perhaps, to a further generation of
heirs. This device safeguarded the bride's jointure, but it had
advantages for the groom's family as well: since the property was held
by a group of feoffees who could co-opt new members and was therefore
immortal, the crown was deprived of its feudal dues on the death of a
tenant-in-chief. These were being insisted upon with greater vigour by
Henry VII (1485–1509) and the entailed use may have owed something
of its popularity from the 1480s to its facility as a means of avoiding
'death duties'. By the same token, lands enfeoffed to the use of the
groom before his marriage would never be held by him according to
common law, and so were not available for the widow's dower. Thus
the entailed use, while guaranteeing jointure, also barred the widow
from claiming her dower, and for this reason has been seen as a reaction
against the generous provision for widows represented by the
combination of jointure and dower.[114]

Villein marriage settlements displayed considerable variety,
depending as they did on a combination of the custom of the manor
and the will and ability of individuals to make their own arrangements.
In 1312 a Derbyshire village bride brought to her marriage 20s. in
cash, a cow (worth 10s.), a dress (worth one mark), and a promise by
her father that he would build a house for the couple to the value of
40s. In 1289 an Oxfordshire father paid his daughter's merchet and
gave chattels to the groom, who in return granted to his father-in-law
the entire profit from his own land for four years, on condition that
the latter kept his son-in-law and, at the end of the term, surrendered
the holding intact and under crop. A Huntingdonshire father in the
early fourteenth century promised to keep his son and daughter-in-
law in his own house or in a house in his courtyard. In 1294 in
Hertfordshire an underage boy was pledged to the daughter of a man
with whom he went to live as his ward. On some manors a form of
jointure settlement could be made. For example, in two early

fourteenth-century settlements made on the manors of St Alban's
Abbey, the groom granted his tenement to the lord, who regranted it
to the bride and groom to hold jointly in survivorship for the term of
their lives, thereafter to remain to the groom's next heir, thereby
allowing the wife to hold it during her widowhood, but without it
passing out of the husband's family forever. Elsewhere, villeins relied
on the custom of the manor, which guaranteed the widow a third, half
or even the entirety of her husband's tenement for her life or until she
remarried, as her freebench, while on some manors she would have
had to relinquish a part of her dower when the son and heir reached
his majority.[115]
  The marriage settlement was reciprocal in that the two families
exchanged property, either transferred more or less immediately, as
dowry, or in the form of a promise of future support for the bride, in
the shape of dower or jointure. Clearly, the bride was allowed certain
rights, and received some benefit from the arrangement, but on
balance, this was not a good deal for her. The dowry was technically a
gift made by the father of the bride to his daughter, but she would
never normally actually have possession of it since it would be
transferred straight from her father to her husband at the time of their
marriage. The character of the dowry as a straightforward gift from
the father is also ambiguous, since in peasant and artisan families the
daughter's own labour would have contributed significantly to the
family resources from which this property was drawn, so that it was in
part the wealth that she had helped to create that was being given to
her husband. Also, in many instances the bride's dowry disqualified
her from any further share in her natal family's property. Finally,
whereas the husband, or his family, had the benefit of the dowry as
soon as it was paid, the wife could only benefit from her dower or
jointure if she outlived her husband, and this eventuality was by no
means certain.[116]

The Ordering of Marriage

The Church recognized three elements to the creation of a legitimate
marriage: betrothal, the announcement of the intended marriage (the
banns) and the blessing in church. This order of marriage was well
established in England by the late thirteenth century.[117] Betrothal was
an expression of the couple's intention to marry, generally made by

the exchange of a vow of future consent (*verba de futuro*), and was roughly analogous to modern engagement. The betrothal was supposed to take place in a suitable place – those betrothed in taverns were to be whipped three times around their parish church – and before reputable witnesses, preferably including a priest.

The second stage of marriage, the reading of banns, was designed to reduce the likelihood of bigamous or incestuous unions being solemnized in church. Before the church blessing the priest was required to make enquiries about the couple's freedom to marry, and to announce their intention of marrying through the reading of the banns, usually on the three consecutive Sundays leading up to the wedding day, and with a saint's day interposed between at least two of the Sundays. If the couple came from different parishes, the banns were to be read in both. Anyone who knew of any impediment to their marriage was obliged to bring this to the priest's attention, or else be in a state of sin and liable to punishment by the ecclesiastical courts.[118]

The third stage, the solemnization in church, consisted of the exchange of vows of present consent (*verba de presenti*) and the blessing of the union by a priest. The church service usually took place on a Sunday morning, when the maximum number of parishioners would have been present, and was held outside of the prohibited seasons of Lent (40 weekdays preceding Easter), Rogationtide (Monday to Wednesday before Ascension Day on the Thursday following Rogation Sunday, the fifth Sunday after Easter Day) and Advent (the four weeks preceding Christmas), which together amounted to about one-third of the year. In Halesowen, May and October seem to have been popular months in which to get married, marking, respectively, the stirrings of Spring and the security of harvest.[119]

The precise ritual surrounding these acts is given in English missals, such as those of Bury St Edmunds, York and Salisbury.[120] The marriage party was met at the church door by the priest, robed in alb and stole and carrying holy water. Here, standing inside the porch, the dower settlement was declared. The significance of the property settlement is suggested by the very name which medieval people gave to this ceremony, for 'wedding' comes from the word wed, meaning a pledge or promise, in this case a promise to provide dower. So important was this most pragmatic and secular aspect of the proceedings that it has come to signify the entire marriage ceremony.[121] The importance of the property settlement is also suggested by the next stage. Tokens of gold and silver, the ring and some pennies, were placed on a book or shield. The pennies were distributed to the poor, while the ring and tokens would be given to the bride later in the service. Next, the priest required those present to declare any known impediment to the marriage. Then the bride was given away by her father or friends and received by the groom, taking her by the right hand. Vows of present consent were then exchanged. One fairly typical set of vows runs as follows:

> *Man*: I take thee N. to my wedded wife, to have and to hold, from this day forward, for better for worse, for richer for poorer in sickness and in health, till death us depart, if holy church it will ordain, and thereto I plight my troth.
>
> *Woman*: I take thee N. to my wedded husband, to have and to hold, from this day forward, for better for worse, for richer for poorer in sickness and in health, to be 'bonere and boxom', in bed and at board, till death us depart, if holy church it will ordain, and thereto I plight my troth.

There is no exact modern equivalent of the Middle English 'bonere and boxom', but in this context it carries connotations both of obedience and of being sexually available to her husband.[122] The ring was then blessed by the priest, who with the groom laid it on each of three fingers of the bride's right hand in honour of the Trinity, before the groom placed it on the third finger of her left hand – through this finger, it was believed, ran a vein that led directly to the heart, the seat of the affections.[123] As he did so, the groom said, 'With this ring I thee wed', and then gave her the gold and silver. According to some versions, the priest said to the groom as he handed this over, 'Lo! This gold and this silver is laid down in signifying that the woman shall have her dower, thy goods, if she abide after thy decease', while the groom said to the bride, 'And with this gold I thee honour'. In some versions, if the bride had been endowed with land, at this point she fell to her knees before her husband. Prayers and blessings followed, after which the marriage party proceeded into the church. Bride and groom prostrated themselves in the nave as more prayers were said over them. They then walked into the choir for the nuptial mass. After the Sanctus the couple prostrated themselves once again and four men placed over them the nuptial veil, also known as pall, or care-cloth. According to the thirteenth-century Bishop Grosseteste, before his time any children born before the marriage were placed under the veil, and by this act were regarded as having been legitimized. At the *Pax* they rose, the groom received the kiss of peace from the priest and passed this on to his bride. The mass concluded with their communion. The priest's final duty was to bless the marriage bed.

The capacious porches of many later medieval churches are a reminder of their importance in the marriage ritual.[124] Significantly, the 'secular' elements of the marriage – the property settlement and exchange of vows – took place in the porch, while most of the sacred elements were reserved for the church interior, in two stages of intensifying sanctity, the first in the nave, the second in the choir, representing the elevation of the union from carnality to sacrament. Immediately after the church ceremony the two families usually returned to one of their homes for a celebratory feast. Inevitably, the combination of heightened emotions and the consumption of alcohol sometimes lead to fighting. In 1268 a fight at a wedding feast at Byram in Yorkshire resulted in many wounded and one fatality. In the case of peasant weddings, one of the lord's agents might attend the feast to remind those present of his right to regulate the marriages of his tenants.[125]

Common to betrothal, banns and blessing was the element of publicity. All three stages were supposed to take place in public, alerting the parish to the impending marriage and requiring anyone with knowledge of an impediment to come forward – even as the couple stood at the church door. These elaborate procedures indicate the scale of the problem of irregular unions. Such unions were either invalid, that is, not marriages at all in the eyes of God, or illicit, in the sense that they were binding unions but constituted in a state of sin. The crucial element in the creation of a valid, but not necessarily legitimate, union was the exchange of vows of present consent between a man and woman who were free to marry each other. The exchange would not constitute a valid union if, for example, the couple were related within the prohibited degrees of consanguinity and affinity, or if one or both was already married. If the couple were free to marry and had exchanged vows *de presenti*, the union was valid and binding (although without two independent witnesses it could not be enforced in a church court), but unless their vows had been made in public, before a priest, and preceded by banns and betrothal, their union was illicit, and as far as the Church was concerned, they languished in a state of sin until their marriage was solemnized in church. Vows could be exchanged anywhere: the location made no difference to their validity. For example, one Hull couple exchanged vows while milking a cow![126]

The mere speaking of words was a perilously easy way to create a permanent, indissoluble union. At no point did canon law attempt to prescribe a precise formula for the vows, thereby leaving tremendous scope for confusion.[127] An example of the form of words that could lead to betrothal is provided by Chaucer's *The Reeve's Tale*. When the young student Aleyn bids farewell to Malyne, the miller's daughter, he tells her:

> Evermore, wherever I walk or ride,
> I am thine own clerk, so have I sworn

Luckily for Aleyn, Malyne did not respond in like terms; had she done so, they would at that moment have become man and wife.[128] The difference between present and future consent could be perilously subtle. Most canon lawyers held that 'I will take you' constituted future consent, but 'I will have you' was a vow of present consent. In case their vows were found to have been of future, rather than present, consent, many suitors before the church courts alleged that sexual intercourse had followed, thereby making their *verba de futuro* a binding contract.[129] That the difference between present and future consent could be so easily misunderstood often had disastrous results. As Pollock and Maitland remarked: 'Of all people in the world, lovers are the least likely to distinguish precisely between the present and future tenses.'[130]

A further complication was presented by the conditional contract. One or both of the parties might make their vows conditional on securing the agreement of their parents. The Church had no objection in principle to this form of conditional contract – indeed, it encouraged couples to marry only with parental consent – but problems arose over the maximum length of time that could be allowed to elapse between vows and the expression of a conditional clause before the latter became invalid. In 1442 the church court at Rochester heard how John Sharp and Joan Broke entered into a marriage contract by *verba de presenti* in a field, but as John and his friends turned to go, Joan called after them, 'Listen, if my master and friends are willing to agree, I will assent to that contract.' John replied, 'You are too late in saying such things. You should have said that sooner.' But when Joan refused to solemnize the marriage and John sued her, the court upheld the condition. Some conditional clauses were deemed invalid because they were incapable of objective verification, such as 'I will take you as my wife if you conduct yourself well', or, as in one Canterbury case, if the woman proved to be a good mother and skilled at brewing, baking and weaving. In both instances it might be argued that the condition could only be realized once the marriage had taken place, thereby making the conditional clause illogical, a similar objection being created by clauses to the effect that the man would only agree to marry if the woman did not commit adultery. Some of these conditional clauses are particularly interesting for what they reveal of one intending spouse's expectations of the other: in the above cases, the grooms wanted well-behaved, good mothers who could make a significant contribution to the household economy. Alice Burden's requirements – as alleged in a Rochester consistory court suit in 1443 – were more basic:

> She confesses that she contracted marriage with him about four years previ-
> ously, under this condition however, that he should be able to act with her
> as a man ought to with a woman. And afterwards within a fortnight, she
> tried him, and because he could not she dismissed him and contracted with
> Thomas Ricard.[131]

Some couples made their exchange of vows *per verba de presenti* and never proceeded to the next stage of a church wedding. They may have chosen a private exchange of vows of present consent because they knew that their union was incestuous or bigamous, or because their parents or feudal lords would prevent them having a legitimate, public marriage. Private marriages which were not designed to lead to a church solemnization may have been practised among some of the poorer members of society, who could not afford a proper church service and for whom, perhaps, the familiar domestic environment was more welcoming than the parish church.

The actual proportion of total marriages contracted without solemnization in church is impossible to determine. The likelihood is that church marriage became more popular at all levels during the later Middle Ages as the teachings of the Church were progressively internalized by lay society. However, it is clear from the records of church courts that the tradition of contracting marriages privately, outside of the church, remained strong until the end of our period, and easily coexisted with church marriage: the great majority of marital suits that came before the church courts concerned marriages that had been contracted outside of church. Clearly, as late as the fifteenth century, many of the laity persisted in the belief that marriages made without benefit of clergy were not only valid – a point which the Church was forced to concede – but also perfectly acceptable. Whether this was a survival of earlier, perhaps even pre-Christian, traditions, or merely stubborn resistance to what was perceived as unnecessary clerical interference is impossible to say, but it seems that by its insistence that any marriage without benefit of clergy was sinful, the Church was seriously out of step with majority lay opinion. The Church's failure to find an alternative to mere consent as the necessary and sufficient constituent of the marriage contract had encouraged the survival of marriages without benefit of clergy, but the difficulty of proving the existence of such unions, combined with the Church's insistence that validly contracted marriages were indissoluble, opened the way to a multitude of misunderstandings, deceits and wrecked lives, as well as giving many canon lawyers a good living.[132]

The ritual surrounding private exchanges of vows does indeed suggest the survival of a vibrant folk tradition of extra-ecclesiastical marriage. Elements of these rituals can be observed in the depositions before ecclesiastical courts: in 1372 a couple exchanged vows sitting on a bench in a York tannery, before kissing between a garland of flowers. Other folk rituals included the giving of rings and the clasping of hands; the latter was so widely practised that 'handfasting' became the common term for such unions.[133] Such marriages would have been regarded as legitimate by their communities, but not by the ecclesiastical authorities, who labelled all unions contracted outside church as 'clandestine'. So-called clandestine marriages need not have been a secret to anyone, including the parish priest. Before an ecclesiastical court in 1471 one Essex man deposed how he was among a group of witnesses

> present in the dwelling-hall of Margery [Mylsent] in the parish of Great Holland ... and William Laykyn, standing, said to Margaret, also standing in the said hall near the doorway toward the highway ... 'Margaret, do you want to have me as your husband?', and she replied 'freely she wanted to have him as her husband, more than ever any woman loved any man ...'[134]

Other 'clandestine' marriages were attended by feasting and the wearing of 'Sunday best'.[135] Such communal celebrations of marriage, or handfastings, fall somewhere between the genuinely clandestine, private exchanges of vows, and the full church wedding. All three forms of marriage may have been contracted successively by some couples, beginning with the private words of consent and ending with the priest's blessing in church. In the church courts, most of the suits to enforce marriages contracted outside of church were brought within two years of the exchange of vows, suggesting that the normal expectation was for the marriage to be solemnized within this period.[136] This was the advice of the reformer Miles Coverdale, who in 1541 recommended that, 'After the handfasting and making of the contract, the church going and wedding should not be deferred too long, lest the wicked sow his ungracious seed in the mean season.'[137] Furthermore, the church court evidence suggests that many private or communal marriages were contracted among those with property and a respected position in local society: the clothing and drink for one village handfasting was alleged to have cost £3 10s. 6d.[138] More surprising, perhaps, is the private exchange of vows made between Sir John Paston and Anne Haute, daughter of a Kentish gentry family. After Sir John had exchanged vows with Anne, his mother, Margaret, reminded him of the solemn nature of their espousal with these words:

> And before God ye are as greatly bound to her as if ye were married, and therefore I charge you upon my blessing that ye be as true to her as if she were married unto you in all degrees.

Their vows seem merely to have been of future consent, but subsequent sexual relations between them turned this promise of marriage into the thing itself. Yet, for Margaret, while her son's union was as binding, it did not of itself amount to a full marriage, a view that would not have been shared by the Church. She was in no doubt that while this was a binding union before God, it was incomplete in the eyes of men.[139] Sir John Paston and his mother had intended his vow to be the first stage in the process that would end with the solemn blessing in church, but this did not happen. Soon, the couple's ardour cooled, or the families no longer wanted the marriage to stand, or both, and it became necessary to acquire a papal dispensation in order to have the union annulled (at one point, Sir John's agent in Rome asked for 1000 ducats in order to secure the dispensation). Did the papal dispensation wipe away all fears that a subsequent marriage would be bigamous, whatever mere mortals might say? Sir John never married – or never married again, to be precise – perhaps, in part at least, because this doubt played on his mind. Others had an even more elastic interpretation of the Church's rules, and believed that *verba de presenti* constituted betrothal rather than a full marriage. Indeed, many couples between exchange of vows of present consent and solemnization referred to themselves as affianced – a relationship perhaps more formal than a modern engagement, but less binding than full marriage.[140] Clandestine marriages – in the sense of any exchange of vows not performed at the church door – were a constant cause of concern for the ecclesiastical authorities. In the consistory court of the diocese of Ely (which was roughly coextensive with the county of Cambridgeshire) between 1374 and 1382, more than 80 per cent of all the marital cases before the bishop's consistory court related to clandestine marriages. A similar proportion has been found in the diocese of Rochester for 1347/8, and in the diocese of Canterbury between 1411 and 1420, 38 out of 41 marital suits concerned unions which had not been solemnized in church.[141] Clandestine marriages raised the spectre of bigamous unions. In the diocese of Ely between 1374 and 1382, 12 suits concerned objections to a proposed marriage raised after the proclamation of banns, and half of these were founded on accusations of pre-contract, and more than 40 per cent of all cases concerned bigamy. One individual was alleged to have contracted up to four bigamous marriages![142] In his study of York consistory court cases, Donahue found that most of the fourteenth-century cases were brought by women, and that most of these were for the enforcement of a marriage contract. Men, he concluded, tended to bring suit when there was a clear economic advantage in enforcing a contract, and dropped suits more readily when the chances of success looked poor; women consequently lost more often than men, sued more often when the financial rewards were less clear, and were less likely to sue to dissolve a marriage. From this, he infers that women took marriage more seriously, or perhaps were more concerned to enforce contracts because most women believed that only marriage could offer them financial security and social status, while men had more options: 'A man could give a woman more by marrying her than she could give him.'[143]

The Church stressed the consequences for the spiritual health of those who entered into a sinful union through a clandestine marriage. These warnings did not necessarily fall on deaf ears. When William Gell boasted to his father of how he had lied before a church court in order to free himself from a clandestine marriage, the latter retorted, 'Son, may it never happen that you so rashly damn your soul. It will be less bad for you to put up with vexation and loathing in your life than after your death to be damnably tortured by the pains of Hell.'[144] For those undeterred, the ecclesiastical courts had a range of options at their disposal. In Ely the consistory court was usually content to make the couple solemnize their union, but in Rochester some offenders were whipped three times around the parish church for contracting clandestine marriages. However, even in Ely harsh punishment was reserved for those couples who, aware of some impediment, married in a parish where both were strangers: this was regarded as a misuse of the sacrament of marriage, and offenders were excommunicated.[145]

As well as the measures available to ecclesiastical courts, the secular courts also acted to discourage clandestine marriages. Common law did not recognize clandestine marriages as creating rights to property and inheritance. Claims to dower and dowry would not be entertained without public solemnization in church, since it was held that only this gave sufficient publicity to the settlement in an age when many such arrangements might be made without written evidence. The children of an unsolemnized union were regarded as illegitimate under the common law, and so might be barred from inheriting their parents' property.[146] In the words of Eric Josef Carlson: 'While consent alone might form a bond in the eyes of God, it must always be viewed in the context of a person's inheritance, whether of paradise or of property.'[147]

2

FAMILY LIFE

Husbands and Wives

The emotional life of all but a handful of medieval people is impossible to reconstruct. They lived in an age when personal feelings were rarely written down, and few of their letters have survived, let alone any diaries or autobiographical accounts. The impression given by the bulk of medieval evidence is of people whose inner lives were dominated by religion, and whose existence in the world was largely determined by the basic needs of survival or by the urge to achieve greater security, wealth or influence. Aside from literary representations, which have their own problems as historical evidence, most of the evidence we have for private life is either of the sort known as normative literature – that is, a text telling people how they should conduct themselves – or emanates from legal or administrative processes. None of this is promising material for the reconstruction of individuals' emotional lives.

Since the appearance of courtly love in eleventh-century France lovers abounded in medieval culture.[1] The classic courtly lover is a young bachelor – the son of a knight or lord – and the object of his love is the wife of his lord. The love should never be consummated, and the dreadful consequences of adultery are demonstrated by the Lancelot and Guinevere story. The young man's unconsummated love leads him to perform heroic feats and undergo fearful dangers and privations, all in the hope of but the slightest sign of reciprocity from the lady. Historians have long debated what relationship, if any, existed between courtly love and affective relationships in the real world. All are agreed that courtly love was not an accurate reflection of reality. Georges Duby, for example, has insisted that courtly love was 'a man's game', the product of a society where the interests of women were regularly sacrificed in the struggle to maintain the family in the male line. For Duby, the reality of courtly love was an educational programme for the young nobleman, designed to bind him ever closer to his feudal lord: the woman was incidental, a cipher. Love, as distinct from lust, between man and woman was in short supply in feudal France: 'Everything therefore conspired to prevent there being a passionate relationship between the married couple comparable to what we regard as conjugal love; instead there was a cold relationship of inequality which consisted at best in condescending love on the part of the husband, and at best timorous respect on the part of his wife.'[2] While the man was free to enjoy an active sex life within and without the marital relationship, his wife was expected to lie back and think of God and her duty to her husband's lineage. While the literature of courtly love is not a mirror held up to the private lives of the Middle Ages, it is difficult to accept that there was no relationship whatsoever between its portrayal of romantic heterosexual love – however flawed this may be in modern western eyes – and real behaviour. Even if the courtly lover and his lady were figments of troubadours' imaginations, the endlessly repeated depictions of such figures must surely have had some influence on the attitudes of the generations of avid consumers of this literature.

Not even the most extreme moralist would have claimed that all sexual activity within marriage was a sin, but the Church did attempt to regulate the practice of marital sexual intercourse. Despite the teachings of St Paul and St Augustine that marriage provided the sole legitimate outlet for sexual desire, much clerical opinion held that sex for any reason other than procreation was to be avoided, since it could not be enjoyed without sin.[3] A man who desired his wife too ardently was no better than an adulterer, and sexual practices designed to avoid procreation were condemned. The only permitted sexual position was that of the man lying on top of the woman: the woman-on-top positions, quite apart from their unwelcome symbolism of female dominance, were condemned since some believed that gravity would prove too much for the sperm, thereby preventing them from reaching the womb.[4]

Whatever qualms it may have had about the carnal aspects of marriage, the Church expected married couples to love one another. In the early twelfth century Honorius of Autun urged: 'Let husbands love their wives with tender affection; let them keep faith with them in all things ... in the same way, women should love their husbands deeply'. A century later, Thomas of Chobham, sub-dean of Salisbury, laid great store by wives' ability to persuade their husbands to virtue: 'When they are alone and she is in her husband's arms, she ought to speak to him soothingly, and if he is hard and merciless and an oppressor of the poor she ought to invite him to mercy'.[5] That Eve was created from Adam's side was taken by some clerics as indicating that women were created as men's companions, neither to dominate (as would be the case if Eve had been taken from Adam's head) nor to be dominated (as would follow if Eve had sprung from Adam's feet), while marital love was sometimes equated with the soul's love for God.[6] According to St Paul, since husband and wife became one flesh, it would be irrational for the husband to do anything other than love his wife, since a man cannot hate his own flesh.[7] Saints' lives sometimes depicted visionary unions between the saint and Mary or Jesus in ways that suggest fantasies of companionship in the context of a mystical marriage.[8]

Moving from clerical exhortation and saintly visions to a real marriage, there can be no doubt of the strength of love between John Paston's sister, Margery, and her husband, the Paston's bailiff, Richard Calle. Between the Pastons' discovery of their clandestine marriage and the family's capitulation about two years later, their enforced separation was deeply painful to them, as Richard's affecting letter to Margery makes clear:

> Meseemeth it is a thousand years ago since that I spoke with you. I had rather than all the goods in the world I might be with you ... I understand, lady, ye have had as much sorrow for me as any gentlewoman hath had in the world, as would God all that sorrow that ye have had had rested on me, so that ye had been discharged of it, for certainly, lady, it is to me a death to hear that ye be entreated otherwise than ye ought to be.[9]

Margery and Richard were not a typical gentry couple. But while John and Margaret Paston may not have been typical either, they were certainly more conventional, and so it is significant that even the businesslike Margaret could write this to her husband when he was recuperating from an illness:

> If I might have had my will, I should have seen you ere this time: I would ye were at home ... now rather than a gown, though it were of scarlet.

To measure her desire to see her husband against the value of a luxury garment is entirely in keeping with Margaret's practical, if not mercenary, personality – and all the more convincing for that.[10] An early fourteenth-century juror told of how the death of his wife had driven him 'almost mad with grief'.[11]

In later medieval France, Christine de Pisan distrusted love as the sole basis for marriage and did not expect it to blossom until some time into the relationship, when the husband's virtues would inspire his wife to love him; she, meanwhile, would support him irrespective of his faults.[12] In this Christine was probably echoing the contemporary elite consensus. Later medieval advice books naturally treat of the relations between husband and wife. *Peter Idley's Instructions to His Son*, written by a fifteenth-century esquire, counsels:

> Thy wife thou love in perfect wise,
> In thought and deed, as heartily as thou can,
> With gentle speech the best thou can devise;
> This shall make her a good woman,
> And also to love thee best of any man,
> And dread thee also and loath to offend,
> Thy goods keep, neither waste nor spend.[13]

In this passage Idley sees conjugal love as a means to an end: by loving his wife the husband can make her a more willing and submissive helpmate who will manage his property the more diligently. Medieval testators valued their wives' managerial abilities, and it is this quality which is most often praised in their wills. Thus, in 1430 Sir Richard Poynings described his wife as 'most diligent and faithful', while phrases such as 'my special trust is in her of all creatures' were common, and it was usual to name one's wife as executor.[14] However, testators' wives were also on occasion accorded warmer epithets, such as 'my most entirely beloved lady and wife'.[15] We cannot know to what extent such expressions were merely common form, and in any case, the infrequency with which they occur should not necessarily be taken as evidence of a general want of affection between spouses. Wills were first and foremost legal documents concerned with the care of the soul and the disposition of property, usually made close to the point of death; assertions of conjugal love were not part of these urgent concerns. On the other hand, testators occasionally took advantage of the licence brought by impending death to unburden themselves of long-harboured grudges. One such was the Derbyshire gentleman John Fitzherbert, whose vitriolic will declares that his wife, 'hath been of lewd and vile disposition and could not be content with me but forsaken my household and company and lived in other places where it pleased her and yet doth to my great rebuke and hers ...'.[16]

Love between man and wife is not necessarily excluded because their marriage has been 'arranged', that is, the union is the product of careful deliberations and negotiation involving their parents, if not also themselves.[17] Among the propertied classes, the frequency of arranged marriages would have made it unrealistic to expect love matches as a general rule – indeed, an outburst of emotional attachment could wreck carefully laid plans – but for the sake of family stability, if for no other reason, a good working relationship between husband and wife was to be encouraged. If this evolved into love, no great harm would be done, provided it did not get out of hand. An arranged marriage at least had the advantage of some degree of compatibility: the couple had something in common, even if it was only the mutual material interests that brought them together in the first place. Marriages based solely on an effervescent passion might lack even that after a short while. Love within an arranged marriage might have been the ideal, but the alacrity with which some propertied fathers negotiated matches between their underage children, sometimes without even specifying which of their children should be chosen as the spouse, not to mention the buying and selling of wardships, does not suggest that the likelihood of personal compatibility was always given serious consideration.

Marriage did not create an equal partnership. The husband was regarded in English law as his wife's lord and master, and this was not simply a form of words. If a husband killed his wife, he would be tried for murder; if the wife killed her husband, she would be tried for petty treason – the penalty for the first was hanging, the second burning at the stake.[18] Accordingly, the wife was expected to be humble and obedient towards her husband. Husbands had the power to inflict corporal punishment on their children, servants, and wives. St Bernardino urged husbands to exercise restraint, not to beat their wives when they were pregnant and, if possible, to use words rather than blows to admonish them; that he had to offer this advice suggests that such brutality was considered only a little beyond the pale.[19]

Wife beating was not universally condemned in medieval England:

> ... a woman to correct is not possible
> With words, except with a staff thou her intreat;
> For he that for a fault his wife will not beat

> Wherein she offended him very much,
> That guider of his house must needs wear no breeches.[20]

An ecclesiastical court accepted that a man accused of twice assaulting his wife with a knife and of breaking her arm was justified on the grounds that she had been disobedient. But the general rule was that loving admonition should be preferred to physical violence. The evidence of royal and manorial courts creates an impression of generalized marital harmony, with complaints of violence between spouses constituting only a tiny minority of cases. However, this impression should be treated with caution. In modern western society only a fraction of marital assaults make it as far as a court of law, either because the victim is unwilling or unable to bring a complaint, or because the authorities are reluctant to intervene in cases of familial violence. There is no reason to believe that there would have been a higher incidence of prosecutions in medieval England. Those cases that do appear in the court records tend to relate to incidents of extreme brutality. For example, one man was accused of beating his wife with a staff so that she died from her injuries. Married women were dependent on their relatives and neighbours to save them from abusive husbands, through communal action or recourse to the law, or both. Direct action had its dangers. The brother of a battered wife found himself charged with murder after felling his brother-in-law with a hatchet after responding to his sister's calls for help as her husband was beating her. Our image of any society would be bizarre in the extreme if we assumed that its law courts provided an undistorted mirror to the lives of the majority, but it seems likely that in general medieval familial relations were attended by a level of violence that was higher and more acceptable – at least to male opinion – than is the case in the western world today.

Women who sought relief from frequent pregnancies, or who simply came to find their husbands physically repellent, might be able to agree to live celibately with their spouses. Sometimes, couples took vows to renounce sexual relations to save their energies for the service of God. Before the twelfth century the Church encouraged lay celibate marriage, perhaps in part as an answer to the problem of clerical marriage or concubinage. Married clergy would be acceptable to an increasingly reformist Church if they took a vow to renounce sexual relations, following the example of the supposedly sexless marriage of Mary and Joseph. Thereafter, lay celibate marriage was discouraged by the Church, perhaps because the outright prohibition of clerical marriage had rendered it unnecessary as a compromise. Also, some clerics might have distrusted it as tempting the celibate laity to regard themselves as their spiritual equals: the elevated status that married women could acquire through remaining celibate would have been particularly troubling.[21] A well-documented, but probably unrepresentative, example is provided by the fifteenth-century East Anglian mystic Margery Kempe. There is no doubting the sincerity of her religious devotion, but a vow of celibacy did solve some problems she had with her marriage, to her satisfaction at least. She did not find her husband attractive, and after 14 difficult childbirths, she called upon Jesus to help her persuade her lusty spouse that he should no longer 'meddle with' her. While on pilgrimage together, Margery told her husband that she would rather see him dead than have sexual intercourse with him. In reply, he offered her a deal: he would consent to her vow of chastity if she would share his bed, eat with him on Fridays, and, last but very probably not least, pay all his debts. She agreed, and dedicated the rest of her life to God.[22]

In theory, the Church made no distinction between male and female adulterers, but in practice the consequences for female adulterers were far graver than for men. The rationalization for this double standard was that name, property and title descended through the male line, and so the proper descent could be disrupted if the child of an adulterous wife and her lover was passed off as the legitimate heir. Despite the Church's dire warnings of its consequences for the soul, adultery may have been common among elite husbands. Some were quite prepared to acknowledge their illegitimate children. The mothers were occasionally from their own social class, but it is likely that more often they were household servants or other lower-ranking women.[23]

Parents and Children

Medieval theorists divided childhood into three parts: infantia, from birth to the age of seven; pueritia, between the ages of seven and 14; and adolescentia, from 14 to the age of majority, which was increasingly regarded as 21.[24] The common law recognized 21 as the age at which males holding by military tenures could enter their estates and administer them independent of parents or guardians. The equivalent for females holding by these tenures was 16 if they were single and 14 if they were married. The disparity between male and female ages was probably the result of the assumption that a girl would remain under the control of an adult male, whether he be her father, guardian or husband. Tenants by socage entered earlier, at 14 or 15. Perhaps the younger ages for landholders by the non-military tenures reflect the original expectation that holders by knight service and serjeanty would normally do actual military service, whereas holders by socage would not. There were other ages at which different responsibilities could be shouldered, however: a boy could make his testament at 14, and a girl at 12; executors could be as young as 17, while a child was regarded as criminally liable after the age of seven.[25] Apart from these staging posts recognized by common law for freeholders, for society in general the defining point came when the young person was married and began to live with his or her spouse as husband and wife. For many daughters, it was at this point that they were transferred from the authority of a father or guardian to that of a husband. Propertied testators were not always happy for their sons to inherit at 21, and stipulated that this crucial moment was to be delayed by three years.[26]

There was a good deal of lore and tradition surrounding childbirth, but little that modern medical opinion would regard as useful practical assistance. Medieval medical writers – almost without exception male – ignored the subject as being the domain of women, and midwives left little evidence of their work. Levels of mortality in the delivery room were very high by modern standards, for both mothers and children. Even among the higher nobility in the later Middle Ages, the infant mortality rate was around 36 per cent for boys and 29 per cent for girls.[27]

Baptism ushered the child into the Christian community. The ceremony was far more than mere symbol. The Church taught that even the unborn carried the burden of original sin, and unbaptized souls would not get to Heaven. With inexorable logic, St Augustine had concluded that unbaptized infants went to Hell, but while such an awful prospect may have been bearable to a saint, it was not something that ordinary sinners could accept with equanimity. From the twelfth century there was a growing belief in Limbo as a destination for these unfortunate souls. The unbaptized would be spared the torments of Hell or Purgatory, but they would never bathe in the Divine light. In the words of Dante:

> There is a place below where sorrow lies

> in untormented gloom. Its lamentations
> are not the shrieks of pain, but hopeless sighs.[28]

To avoid this fate, the baby was baptized soon after it had been born, or even while it was still in the birth canal if the midwife thought it was likely to be stillborn. In such extreme circumstances, the sacrament of baptism could be administered by a member of the laity – often the midwife, although the thought of a lay woman administering the sacrament caused disquiet among some clerics. When the baby was judged likely to survive long enough for a church ceremony, the midwife would tie the umbilical cord and wash the child in warm water, sometimes with the addition of oil, salt, rose petals or perhaps even milk or wine. The baby's limbs would be straightened, and it was then ready for its first set of swaddling clothes. Babies were tightly wrapped in swaddling (strips of linen or woollen material), partly to keep them warm, but also as a means of restraint. For toddlers, this was obviously a useful way of keeping the infant out of harm's way when there was no adult available to watch over it, but swaddling was believed to be beneficial to the newborn, whose limbs, it was thought, needed to be kept straight or else they would grow crooked.[29]

Meanwhile, the father would send for the godparents to attend the baptismal ceremony in the parish church. Even if the child looked healthy, baptism was carried out as quickly as possible, just in case it died without warning. The baptism ceremony, initiating the child into life as a Christian, had certain similarities with the solemnization of marriage, the second great religious rite of passage. As in the marriage ceremony, those things associated with human carnality had to be kept at a distance from the sacred. The child was brought to the church in procession by the godmother or midwife (its mother could not enter a church until her churching, or purification), and the party was met by the priest at the church door. Here certain preliminary safeguards were put in place. The priest ascertained the child's sex, name and the identity of its godparents, and established that it had not already been baptized. Before entering the church, the child was blessed and exorcized. Only then could this creature be allowed into a hallowed space. Up to this point, the baby had been completely unprotected not only from the consequences of original sin, but also from demonic possession. Having taken these elementary precautions, the baptismal party proceeded to the font. Here they prayed as the child was anointed, immersed, named and then wrapped in the white christening robe which the church usually provided for the occasion. The holy water in the font was precious, and priests were instructed not to change it too regularly: water into which a child had urinated was not considered too sullied to be used again. In the final stage of the ceremony, the child was taken to the altar where the profession of faith was made, the godparents taking the child's part.[30]

Most children would have been named after a relative, saint or godparent. If the godparents of two brothers or two sisters shared the same first name, then the parents might have two sons called John, or two daughters called Margaret.[31] Godparents, then as now, were expected to ensure that their godchildren were instructed in the basics of Christianity – the *Pater Noster*, *Ave Maria*, and *Credo* – and were also charged with arranging the child's confirmation. Each child was supposed to have three godparents: for boys, two men and a woman; for girls, two women and a man. Sometimes, godparents were chosen from a higher social rank than the parents, in the hope that they would act as patrons in the baby's later life.[32]

Because baptism ceremonies could not be delayed until elaborate preparations had been made, the main celebration of a birth usually took place afterwards. Often, a feast was held 40 days after the birth, following the mother's churching, when she was ritually purified, allowing her to enter church.[33] The feast might be lavish, involving a wide circle of relatives, neighbours and friends. Gift giving seems to have been a common part of the ritual surrounding childbirth, and there are records of game, cattle and money being given to mothers and babies, and also of swords, bows and arrows, and cattle given to guests at feasts. Apart from marking the child's entry into the community, such public celebrations served to reinforce the memory of its birth in the minds of those who might one day be called upon to testify to the year of its birth, thereby establishing that the child had attained its majority and so could enter its inheritance. Memory was often the only means of determining the date of birth in an age before parish registers. The motive is made explicit in the testimony of Peter Fitzwarin in 1309, who claimed that he could remember the date of birth of an heir 'because Warin the father came to Wermenstre on the fifteenth day after the heir's birth and held a feast there, where the witness was present and was asked to give testimony to the day and year of the birth of the heir when he should come to full age'.[34] When the heir to a noble or gentry family was born, the church bells might be rung, and people would be encouraged to celebrate in the streets, providing a similarly memorable event. Jurors in inquisitions to prove the age of an heir often determined the year in which the heir was born by reference to the birth of their own children; significantly, the birth of sons was remembered far more often than daughters, suggesting that a baby boy would have been far more welcome than a girl, and therefore more memorable.[35]

Infants spent much of their time swaddled, but even swaddled in their cradles, babies were at risk when left unattended in homes where animals could wander about with apparent ease, and the coroners' rolls tell several stories of babies being bitten by pigs or dogs as they lay in their cradles.[36] That toddlers were not kept permanently swaddled is demonstrated by melancholy stories of infants wandering into the road and being crushed by passing wagons, pulling pots of boiling liquid over themselves or falling into fires and streams. Wetnurses were employed by the elite, but for everyone else they were only resorted to when the mother was dead or incapable of giving milk. In any case, the hiring of a wetnurse would have been beyond the means of most families. Before pasteurization, the use of animal milk posed serious health risks for the baby, and it was not generally favoured in the Middle Ages, so that a wetnurse was often the only alternative where a mother could not, or would not, breast-feed her own child. Moralists regularly decried those mothers who employed wetnurses, but the Church's hostility appears to have had little effect on elite opinion and practice. Nursing mothers were urged not to have sexual intercourse, since it was believed that semen could poison the milk, and pregnancy while nursing can endanger the milk supply. Lactation also depresses female fertility, and so the effect of maternal nursing is to restrict the frequency of pregnancy. This was particularly so in medieval England, where infants were usually only weaned around the age of two. This is probably the reason behind the elite fashion for employing wetnurses, despite the likelihood that a wetnurse would not nourish the child as well as its mother. Thus, the slight reduction in the individual child's chances of survival was offset by the mother's ability to produce more offspring. A wetnurse could either live in the parental household, or could nurse the child in her own home. Wetnurses had suffered the early death of their own baby, had given it away, or attempted to feed both their own and their employer's children.[37]

By the age of two or three peasant girls were accompanying their mothers as they went about their household chores, such as cooking, gathering food and drawing water from wells; boys likewise spent much of their time in the home, but they also watched their fathers at work beyond the homestead. An occupational gender divide is thus already apparent at this young age. By four or five children were beginning to cross the boundary between play and work, being sent to bring water or used as baby-sitters, although the wise mother tried not to entrust her baby to the care of such a young child.

From seven to 12 lower-rank children began to make a significant contribution to the household economy. Boys are recorded fishing, gathering fuel and food, tending livestock, carrying messages and doing errands, and assisting with thatching and harvesting. Girls also gathered food and helped their mothers drawing water, building fires, cooking and laundering. Among the children of craft, mercantile and landed families, this was the time when they began learning the skills they would need in adult life, but in their case, this was done as part of more formal education and training. However, many wealthier peasants gave at least one son a basic education. Manorial lords generally charged their villeins a fine for allowing their sons to attend school. Among the elites, both sexes would learn etiquette, boys and many girls would have at least basic instruction in literacy and numeracy, and noble and gentry boys learnt how to ride and handle weapons.

During adolescence individuals gradually took on the adult roles regarded as appropriate to their gender. Males in peasant families spent more time in the fields, but were still less likely to be involved in skilled activities. Adolescent males spent more time around the home than they would as adults. Most teenage girls had to make a less dramatic transition, since they would tend to continue to spend much of their working lives within the home environment.

Parental discipline was often harsh, with corporal punishment being regularly meted out. In the fifteenth century, the advice of Agnes Paston to the tutor of her 15-year-old son Clement, a student at Cambridge, was that, 'if he hath not done well, nor will nought amend, prey him that he will truly belash him till he will amend.'[38] Hanawalt found no instances in the coroners' rolls where jurors intervened to stop a child-beating, but there are chilling stories of children being beaten to death by their parents. Even by the harshest standards, such rare cases would be regarded as abusive and their perpetrators as criminals.[39]

There was a softer side to parenthood. Saints' lives sometimes relate how their subjects had visions of maternal intimacy with the infant Christ, suckling him or helping his mother bathe him. The cult of Mary came to dominate later medieval popular piety, and its central feature was her relationship with her infant son. This aspect of the cult has left us a tangible legacy in the countless painted and sculpted portrayals of the Madonna and child. As early as 994 Bernard of Anjou wrote of the rearing of children: 'For it is the natural bent of all human beings to believe that in this lies the largest part of their happiness.'[40] A mid-fourteenth-century confessor's manual assumed 'that parental love conquers every other love'.[41] Among the many expressions of medieval parental love is the testimony of an early fourteenth-century juror who described how his son had drowned in a well, 'on account of which his mother was sick for half a year following'.[42] Contrary to the opinion of Philippe Ariès, medieval parents did, by and large, love their children, and both mothers and fathers took an active interest in their development.[43]

Peter Idley promised to help his son if he conducted himself 'in virtue with good intent', but,

> ... if thou do the contrary, trust me well,
> I will put from thee without nay
> Land and goods everydeal
> And all that ever I goodly may;[44]

The evidence from wills and other legal documents may suggest that parents distrusted their children when it came to the management of property. Propertied fathers often made bequests to their children conditional on the latter's obedience. For example, in Edmund Chertsey's will of 1474, his son and daughter were left money so long as they 'be guided and governed by my wife their mother and if they do contrary I will they have none.'[45] We cannot know how often these clauses were the product of genuinely poor relations between parents and children, or merely the safeguards recommended by lawyers.[46]

Family Size

Determining the average size of households is one of the most difficult problems facing historians of the medieval family. Medieval surveys such as Domesday Book or the fourteenth-century poll taxes tended to concentrate on the head of the household and under-recorded other household members and, in any case, did not record every household. This means that in order to arrive at a figure for the total number of persons living within an average household, the number given in the source material has to be multiplied. The multiplier is determined by educated guesswork, based on comparative evidence and logical deduction. Not surprisingly, this process has been the subject of considerable debate among historians, and widely differing estimates have been offered for the average size of the medieval English household. However, recent work has tended to settle on an average of between four and five persons for later medieval peasant households. The figure tends to be higher for households before the Black Death than after it, and higher for wealthier families. For example, at Kibworth Harcourt in Lincolnshire, Howell found an average household size of 4.84 before 1348, but only 3.72 afterwards. In pre-plague Halesowen, the richer peasants had on average 5.1 children, the middling peasants 2.9, and the poorest only 1.8; but after the plague the average number of children for Halesowen families dropped to 2.1. In thirteenth-century Lincolnshire the average family size for richer peasants was 6.2, dropping to 4.78 for the middling sort and 4.33 for the poorest. Family size tended to increase with wealth, since wealthier parents generally enjoyed better living conditions, better health, higher fertility and a higher survival rate for their children. In addition, the size of their households was more likely to have been increased by the existence of servants.[47]

Some caveats are necessary to this near-consensus. The tendency for some married heirs-apparent to live in a separate household but on their father's holding, and the occurrence of arrangements whereby retired or widowed parents lived in separate houses within their son's holding, means that what are counted as two households may, in fact, have functioned as one. In addition, a mean figure, produced by dividing the total number of persons by the number of households, does not, of course, imply that most, let alone all, lived in the ideal household produced by this calculation. Many lived in larger households, and many lived in smaller.[48] Naturally, some couples did not produce children, and many more were not survived by their children. In pre-plague Halesowen, 13 per cent of tenants died childless, but from 1350 to 1400, the figure leaps to a staggering 39 per cent.[49] Other households were made up of single people, widows or widowers. This has a bearing on what contemporaries would have regarded as the ideal size of family: we should not assume that the mean family size was what was aimed at by medieval parents, since the figure was influenced by single-person households or couples who had failed to produce surviving children – surely not an ideal situation – and so a household of only four to five might well have been regarded as small. English peasant houses were insubstantial and relatively easy to build. This made it unnecessary for kin beyond the conjugal unit to share one house, since basic accommodation for each couple could usually be provided, albeit often at a very basic level. There seems little evidence for co-resident extended families as the norm in medieval England, at least in the strict sense of two couples sharing one roof. This is supported by the more plentiful early modern evidence, which has been used to demonstrate that the characteristic English family, from the sixteenth century onwards, has been simple, or nuclear.[50]

In the later Middle Ages at least, most couples had no more than four children who survived beyond infancy: in other words, these families were not significantly larger than is normal in modern western society. Today, family size is limited by late marriage, the use of contraception and abortion, and, to a lesser extent, by the early termination of marriage through divorce, although if this is followed by remarriage it may have little effect on the number of children produced by the two individuals in their total lifetimes. How was medieval family size limited?

Age at first marriage has an important impact on family size. The later the age of first marriage, the less time there is in which to produce children, and so the smaller the family size. As we have seen, most people in later medieval England married in their early or mid-twenties: broadly comparable with trends in modern western society. The number of separations or annulments in medieval society was probably not statistically significant, but in some ways the place occupied by divorce in the contemporary West was taken in the Middle Ages by death: remarriage is common to both societies, but in the one its precondition is provided by divorce, in the other by the death of the previous spouse leaving the survivor still young enough to marry again. Life expectancy is determined by a range of factors, including socioeconomic position and the prevalence of epidemic disease. Ferociously high rates of medieval infant mortality mean that any calculation of life expectancy based on survival rates from birth will give a very low figure. An alternative technique is to calculate average life expectancy from some later point in the life-cycle. Often, in the absence of baptismal registers, this is, in any case, all we can do.

The five-year-old child of a ducal family in later medieval Britain could have expected to live for about another 40 years.[51] In Kibworth

Harcourt, male peasants could expect to live another 28 years from
the point at which they entered their holdings, which on average took
place around the age of 25. Therefore average male life expectancy
for those who had survived childhood and adolescence was about 53: a
perfectly respectable age at any time in English history before the later
nineteenth century. At the time of the 1379 poll tax returns, over a
quarter of Kibworth Harcourt couples had been married for over 25
years, and over half had been married for 16 years or more. The impact
of epidemic disease is revealed from the Kibworth Harcourt data when
the average life expectancy of those who had died of plague is compared
with the rest: for the latter, the figure is 32 years from the point at
which the individual entered his lands; for those who died of plague,
the figure is a mere 20.8.[52] Periods of severe famine may also have had
an effect on mortality rates, particularly among the poor. Disease is
more democratic, but not entirely disrespectful of rank, since the rich
were generally better nourished, better housed and more mobile,
enabling them to flee from plague-stricken areas.[53] Even in late
fourteenth- and fifteenth-century conditions of unusually high
mortality, most couples had about 15 years of married life. On average,
they managed to produce fewer than three surviving children in those
15 years. Even allowing for the possibility of marginally younger average
ages of menopause and lower female fertility through malnourishment,
this shows that the length of marriage does not of itself explain the
small size of the medieval family.[54]

To what extent did medieval couples make deliberate efforts to limit
the number of their offspring? Contraception is by its nature a private
matter and, when condemned as sinful, its practitioners take care to
conceal their use of it still further, so it is probably impossible to arrive
at any firm conclusions about its extent in medieval England. There is
some evidence of women using drugs and suppositories to prevent
procreation, or to induce a miscarriage, and it may be that from the
thirteenth century, the greater knowledge of Greek and Roman
practices led to an increasing use of contraceptive techniques among
the elite, but for the majority it is probably the case that folk recipes
were passed down through the generations. The most widely employed
means of contraception seems to have been coitus interruptus. The
medieval Church equated coitus interruptus with the Sin of Onan in
Genesis, and condemned it accordingly, along with all other practices
designed to prevent procreation – even abstinence if it was motivated
not by a genuine devotion to God, but by the desire to avoid producing

children. The Christian tradition did not draw a sharp distinction between abortion and contraception. Abortion was not always regarded as homicide. There was a widespread belief that the soul was incarnated into the foetus not at the moment of conception, but 40 days afterwards; thus, it could be argued that abortion before the soul entered was not homicide. This was the position of the Roman Catholic Church until 1917. There are few instances of infanticide allegations. Hanawalt's analysis of coroners' rolls has found that the circumstances of most infant deaths are more readily explicable in terms of accident rather than design. Strong folk traditions stressed the awful consequences of infanticide, indicating that it was not regarded as an acceptable form of family limitation. Sex ratios – the proportion of males to females – appear to have been reasonably close, and this is not the pattern one would expect if parents regularly exposed or seriously neglected female babies in preference to male.[55]

However, seasonal cycles of births suggest that some form of family planning was practised, even if it was only abstinence, perhaps to avoid pregnancies and childbirth at inconvenient times of the year, such as harvest when women would be required to work in the fields. In the early Middle Ages, the Church taught that abstinence should be observed on certain holy days, during menstruation, during pregnancy and for periods after childbirth, with the result that the pious couple determined to follow these rules to the letter would have had little more than 80 days in the year when they could have had sexual intercourse. Canonical periods of abstinence were less strictly adhered to in the later Middle Ages.[56] An increasing number of references in later medieval texts condemning attempts at contraception and abortion, as well as sodomy (defined as any form of penetration other than virginal) may represent either the greater use of these techniques, or merely a greater concern among clerics and moralists.

Lactation would have had some effect on fertility. During the two years or more that most mothers breast-fed their babies their fertility would have been reduced, and common assumptions about the contaminating effects of sperm on mothers' milk may have persuaded some husbands to practise sexual restraint during this nursing period. The employment of wetnurses by wealthier parents may partly explain why their families tended to be larger.[57] However, once again this cannot be more than a contributory factor, since it does not explain the drop in family size after the Black Death: nursing practices are unlikely to have changed either side of 1348.

Infant mortality is one factor which has changed dramatically since the Middle Ages. Infant mortality rates approaching 40 per cent – perhaps even higher during outbreaks of plague – must have had a significant impact on family size. This factor fits well with the variations in family size related to socioeconomic position and chronology noted above. The better living conditions of wealthier families would presumably have lessened somewhat their incidence of infant mortality. In the period after the Black Death, while improved living conditions for the survivors would have increased their resistance to disease, some of the subsequent epidemics seem to have struck at children with particular virulence. The infant death-toll combined with the relatively short duration of married lives to limit family size. After the Black Death, people married later and infant mortality rose, reducing the rate at which the population could reproduce itself, and thereby delaying demographic recovery until the very end of the fifteenth century.[58]

There is a difference between family size – in the sense of the number of children produced who survive beyond infancy – and household size, defined as the number of people living together under the same roof at a given moment. Household size is not determined simply by the number of surviving children produced, since some may have left their parents' home in search of employment or to marry and found another household, and there may also be other kinsfolk, servants or lodgers living under the same roof as the head of household.

Leaving Home

The adolescent's decision to stay at home or seek a fortune among strangers may sometimes have been influenced by the quality of relationships within the family. As we know from modern western society, for some even a precarious existence on the streets is preferable to remaining within an abusive and hostile family environment, and children are sometimes not given the option of staying at home. In all cases, however, economic factors would have been considered, and the balance between the opportunities offered by the family holding and those available elsewhere was often the main or sole deciding factor. The more prosperous peasant households might be able to find work for younger sons and daughters by buying more land within the village or by hiring fewer labourers. Those who could not afford this were faced with a stark choice: either divide their existing meagre resources between more mouths or encourage their excess offspring to go elsewhere.[59] But the latter option is only satisfactory if alternative employment exists. In periods of extreme pressure on resources this may not have been the case, and then the very real prospect of having to scratch a living by begging, casual labour or crime would have encouraged all but the most impoverished, foolish or abused to remain at home. This is brought out starkly by Howell's comparison of peasant household composition in Kibworth Harcourt either side of the Black Death: the 1280 tithing lists reveal 'a deep reservoir of brothers and sons awaiting land'; by 1377–9 the poll tax evidence suggests that 'the able-bodied had for the most part left the village to seek their fortunes in a buoyant labour market.' For many, their first employment beyond their home parish was as a servant. In Kibworth Harcourt the poll tax returns appear to reveal a significant number of males who had been absent from the village between the age of about 14 and their early twenties, which suggests that they had been working as servants in nearby villages and towns. Presumably a significant number did not return to be counted for the poll tax in their parents' households, but married and settled down elsewhere.[60]

This pattern of adolescent mobility was part of a more general trend that appeared in Kibworth Harcourt after the Black Death. During the 60 years from 1280 to 1340, no families left the village or ceased holding land and only five new families entered, but by 1390 only about 16 families had been resident for any significant period, and this figure had halved 50 years later. This rapid turnover of families was partly a consequence of family extinction through higher mortality, but also a reflection of the greater opportunities available for the survivors of the recurrent epidemics. Land was plentiful, labour at a premium and feudal controls on mobility beginning to break down.[61] A broadly similar pattern has been observed in Halesowen. Before the Black Death most children remained on the manor, many newly married sons setting up house on their father's tenement, some even sharing their father's house. From 1350 onwards, married children no longer clustered around their parents' holdings, and many more moved off the manor.[62]

There appear to have been regional variations from this pattern. In Halesowen, Razi found that the number of sons entering land before their fathers' death or retirement increased after the Black Death, and he concluded that 'practically every young villager who reached the age of twenty and wished to settle in Halesowen acquired a holding without any difficulty.'[63] This still leaves the question of how many would want to remain in their home village when there were ample opportunities elsewhere.

A new rift opened between parents and children after the Black Death. The older generation wanted at least their heirs to remain on the family holding: whatever emotional attachment the parents might have had to the lineage (if not to their children), there was the very practical matter of who was to support them in their old age. In this desire they were joined by their lords, who prized continuity in their tenancies, since any vacant holdings could not produce rents and dues. The children, on the other hand, had constantly before them the temptations of cheap land elsewhere, free of parental control and available on attractive terms from lords desperate for labour. There was also the prospect, not entirely illusory, of becoming a Dick Whittington in the nearest large town. An increasing number of peasants flouted manorial controls in search of greener pastures, encouraged by other lords who, by offering good terms to runaway villeins, put their need for labour before solidarity with others of their class. This situation created a new relationship between family and property: 'The very premise on which the medieval inheritance system had operated – that inheritance was by far the best means of acquiring land, while alternative livelihoods were scarce – was now nullified, and was to remain so for over a century.'[64]

Servants

For many young people, adolescence was spent as a household servant, and this often entailed moving out of their home village. While many were drawn to the larger towns and cities, most probably travelled only about 20 miles to their new home.[65] In medieval usage, 'servant' denoted anyone employed to provide labour for a family and given lodging within that family's household. Thus the key defining characteristic of servants, as opposed to labourers, was not the nature of their work, but their residence with their employers. Most servants were young and single, entering service from the age of 12 and remaining as servants until their mid- or occasionally late twenties. Most servants served for a year at a time, and were probably hired from Michaelmas (29 September) to Michaelmas in southern England, and from Martinmas (11 November) to Martinmas in the North. Hiring fairs may have taken place at these times, as they did in early modern England, but employers often recruited their servants from within their own kin, neighbourhood or trade. Servants were often related to their masters. Inevitably, the proximity between master and servant could sometimes lead to abuse, and female servants would have been particularly vulnerable to the sexual advances of their masters. Another form of abuse was the excessive use of violence against servants. Here the situation was very similar to that regarding children: a certain level of corporal punishment was acceptable, even recommended, but there were limits, and there are cases of servants' contracts being dissolved by a court which had been persuaded of their unacceptably violent treatment at the hands of their masters. However, there is also ample evidence of good relations between master and servant, and it is likely that some servants were retained for periods of several years. The significant number of servants remembered in their masters' or mistresses' wills are likely to have been in this category. Indeed, where family relationships were distant, it is likely that a long-standing servant might have provided greater companionship, and perhaps truer friendship, than one's immediate family.[66]

The Black Death and subsequent epidemics reduced the number of children who survived to the age at which they could make a significant contribution to the family economy, and where there was insufficient family labour to work a holding or family business, labour had to be hired.[67] But the demographic downturn had made wage labour more expensive, and it has been suggested that residential servants became a more economical source of labour as a result, since a large part of their remuneration came from board and lodging rather than wages. On the basis of the later fourteenth-century poll taxes, it appears that about one-sixth of rural and one-third of urban households kept servants. A combination of labour shortages and the cheaper rates at which women could be hired may have encouraged the greater employment of young women as household servants. In towns at least, most of these female servants, particularly from the mid-fifteenth century, were probably employed as unskilled general domestics rather than as workers in crafts or trade. The greater opportunities for employment may in turn have presented young women with a more attractive alternative to marriage.[68]

In towns, servants joined with apprentices and children among the young dependants of the head of household. Like servants, apprentices were young and unmarried. The vast majority were male. The difference between the two groups was that apprentices were contracted to their masters by their families on the understanding that they would be trained in their master's craft. The apprentice's family paid a fee to the master for this training, and in return for this and his service the apprentice received board and lodging with his master. The periods of apprenticeship were much longer than the average year for which a servant contracted. Youths entered their apprenticeships at ages ranging from 12 to 16. The length of apprenticeship varied according to the craft or trade; generally speaking, the more prestigious occupations demanded longer apprenticeships. In early Tudor Coventry, apprentice carpenters served for five years, as against the apprentice drapers' and grocers' nine. Apprenticeships with the more prestigious trades were also more expensive. With some apprentices not completing their terms until their mid-twenties, apprenticeship, like service, delayed the average age of first marriage.[69]

Household service was itself a form of apprenticeship, training youths for their adult roles.[70] This was as true of the elite as it was for the rest of society. There was no sense of disparagement about the son or daughter of a gentleman acting as a servant in a noble household; quite the reverse, since the gentle servants of a great magnate shared in his prestige. Up to one-third of the servants in later medieval magnate households were gentle-born. Gentry families, such as the fifteenth-century Pastons of Norfolk or the Stonors of Oxfordshire, were keen to place their adolescent children in service with a great household, where they could learn the etiquette and fashions of their social betters, make useful contacts, and perhaps even meet their future spouses.[71] They had plenty of opportunities to meet people, since magnate households could be vast.

The household of Thomas, Earl of Lancaster in 1318–9 comprised over 700 people: while some of these were guests or paupers kept within the household, the majority would have been servants of one form or another. A crucial distinction was drawn between what we would today call 'above stairs' and 'below stairs' servants: the latter carried out the menial tasks such as food preparation, cleaning and laundering, were recruited from the lower orders, and were usually employed for periods of a year at a time; the former appeared in the lord's presence, waited on his person, were often drawn from the ranks of the gentry, and might continue serving in the same household for a period of years. Upper servants might follow their fathers and grandfathers in service to the same noble family. The gentry themselves could be substantial employers of servants. The household of Sir John Scott, in fifteenth-century Kent, was said to contain 60 servants. At the other end of the scale, the Kentish gentleman William Brent (d. 1496) had a household that probably consisted of himself, his wife and four children, and only six servants. Most servants in noble and gentry households were male. For much of the Middle Ages this was because lords looked to their households to provide them with a core of armed men for their protection, the intimidation of their enemies, and to help meet the military demands of their superior lords. The size of noble households seems to have declined during the fourteenth and fifteenth centuries, perhaps as lords found more convenient ways of maintaining their influence and meeting their commitments. However, while the proportion of female and young servants increased, great households continued to have a strongly masculine character up to and beyond the end of our period.

Great households changed in other ways. As domestic life became more sophisticated, with greater stress on comfort, the elaboration of ritual and the increasing separation between the family and their servants, so the gradations of age, status and function among the servants became more pronounced. During the fourteenth and fifteenth centuries boys and adolescents appear as, respectively, pages and grooms. Young men known as footmen and henchmen accompanied the lord on journeys; the former were employed to run alongside the riders, ready to hold their bridles when they came to dismount; the latter seem to have been gentle-born, and served as part of their education and training. As the lord and his family increasingly lived their daily lives in semi-private apartments, they employed specialist body servants, also of high rank, to attend to their more intimate needs, while the later medieval penchant for tight-fitting clothes meant that the fashionable noble required help in dressing.

Household service was a common experience for young people at most levels of society, from peasants to princes. While there was a small number of 'professionals' who remained in service for all or most of their working lives, most were 'life-cycle' servants spending their adolescence in service. As well as providing both support for youths who were excess to their families' labour requirements and labour to their employers, the institution of service played an important part in socializing young people, training them in the social and craft skills necessary for their adult existence. Service also fostered links between families and across socioeconomic boundaries. Finally, the impact of

increased opportunities for female employment in service may have
had a crucial impact on the demographic profile of England after the
Black Death.

Kinship

In determining an individual's social identity, the Anglo-Saxons did
not give special significance to the lineage. Collateral, horizontal
relationships – between siblings, for example – were at least as important
as vertical ones between parents and children. One expression of this
is that family names, or patronymics, were not customary: personal
names did not signify that a person's relationship to their lineage was
more important than other kinship relationships.[72] Anglo-Saxon
kinship terms generally were few and undifferentiated beyond the
nuclear family, perhaps indicating that kinship was not central to
determining an individual's social identity. The Normans added
'cousin', 'uncle' and 'aunt', but Middle English continued to lack a
wide vocabulary of kinship, perhaps indicating the lesser importance
of wider kin groups. A far more significant Norman introduction was
the tendency to promote the lineage over collateral kin. By the late
thirteenth century, family surnames were in general use and fairly stable
among the majority of the English elite, although for the rest family
names continued to show some fluidity into the sixteenth century.[73]
The lineage did not overshadow collateral relationships completely.
While lineage was more important than collateral relationships among
the Anglo-Norman nobility, the lineage in England was never as strong
as it was in France: in England, men and families came and went from
the ranks of the nobility according to their wealth and office holding,
preventing the development of a noble caste based exclusively on blood
on the French model. The Anglo-Norman nobility maintained a
meaningful attachment to their kinfolk beyond the nuclear family, so
that, in the words of Professor Holt: 'The kin constituted a mutual
benefit society of a very material kind and that over a far wider range
of relationships than those likely to arise in a straightforward descent
of estates.'[74] However, nobles exercised discretion in their choice of
kin with whom they did business, and nor did they restrict themselves
to relatives: neighbourhood, friendship and seigneurial relationships
all provided alternatives, and among their kin it was still the most
immediate – parents, children and siblings – who formed the main

focus of solidarity.[75]

Most historians are now agreed that in later medieval England, if not earlier, the characteristic family was nuclear, in the sense that relatives beyond parents and their children did not usually share the same roof. Extended co-resident families were not a common feature of later medieval or early modern English society: couples did not usually marry until they could support a separate establishment, and parents seldom lived long enough to make three-generational families anything more than short-lived phenomena. There is a partial exception in the case of elite families, where people tended to live longer, had more children, and had more space in which to accommodate parents, in-laws and other relatives beyond the nuclear family, but such families made up a small minority of the population.[76]

However, Razi has urged that a distinction should be drawn between co-resident extended families and 'functional' extended families. By the latter is meant the wider kin group to which the nuclear family habitually looks for companionship, material aid and emotional support. While the nuclear family seems to have been a persistent characteristic of English society, there may have been variations in the significance of the functional extended family depending on time and place. Razi suggests that before the Black Death, in the greater part of central southern, Midlands and northern England most land was distributed through inheritance and marriage, with the land market functioning largely for the transfer of the odd acre of land rather than entire holdings. Most villagers, while not being entirely immobile, had strong links with their birthplace. The result was that in a given community there was a good deal of interrelationship, or high kin density, and functionally extended families predominated. Elsewhere, in the more densely settled and economically diverse East Anglia, south-east and south-west England, holdings tended to be smaller, more fragmented, and bought and sold more intensively in a more dynamic property market. Manorial control was less pronounced. The population was much more mobile. The result was low kin density, a lesser incidence of functionally extended families and more pronounced nuclear families, with a less tenacious grasp on inherited land. Before the twelfth century the former pattern was perhaps common across England. After the Black Death, but particularly after the 1430s, the combination of higher mortality and increased mobility acted as a solvent to kin density and the extended functional family: land was less often transferred within the kin group, which was also less often relied upon for support and welfare. Apart from one or two isolated pockets, from the mid-fifteenth century family structure and kin relations became more homogeneous across England. The more fluid and dynamic land market that resulted in turn encouraged the socioeconomic polarization of the peasantry, giving rise to the consolidation of the yeoman class and the growing capitalization of agriculture.[77] Such a model helps to explain variations in the intensity of extended kin relationships noticed in different parts of the country. For example, in the manorial court of Redgrave in thirteenth-century East Anglia, only 10.7 per cent of transactions involved kin, while in the Midlands manor of Halesowen, over 46 per cent of interactions recorded in the court were between kin beyond the nuclear family.[78]

Some of the manorial court transactions counted as evidence of kinship interactions were the result of conflict, and relations between kinsfolk were not always amicable. In particular, it is not uncommon to find the children of a first marriage suing their step-parents over property. For example, Emma Mabyll, daughter of a wealthy peasant family, had a son, Richard, by her first husband, and then married Adam de Sutton, who persuaded her to sell the property that Richard regarded as his inheritance. Richard killed Adam with a staff in front of his mother. Siblings might also fall out. In Halesowen in 1323, Henry Snode had his brother John's holding confiscated on the grounds that he was a bastard; John was also fined for assaulting their mother with a knife and calling her a 'bytch'. On the other hand, one fourteenth-century juror spoke of his deceased brother, whom he had 'loved above all living'. Networks of kin and neighbours may have acted as some kind of constraint on family violence, with a particularly brutal husband being exposed and publicly criticized by his wife's kin and friends.[79]

The nature and significance of kinship relations varied according to gender and rank. Married women were usually distanced from their natal kin. Brides married into new families, bridegrooms remained in their families of birth. The late-medieval practice whereby women changed their family name when they married was an eloquent symbol of the reality faced by married women. Judith Bennett's work on Brigstock before the plague has shown how women had to leave behind the family of their birth in favour of their husband's kin, while husbands not only maintained their own family network, but also tended to associate with the kin of their wives. Coping with the emotional strains of this transition must often have been difficult for wives, particularly if the husband already had a family by a previous wife.[80]

Since Anglo-Norman times, a sense of lineage was probably strongest among the landed classes. The importance of dynasty is revealed in several aspects of noble and gentle life, including the use of heraldic arms and tomb sculptures to express an individual's relationship to the kin group in general, and the lineage in particular. The two methods are combined in the will made in 1496 by John Pympe, a Kentish esquire. He ordered that his tomb should carry an account of his lineage stretching back over five generations, while in the windows of his burial church should be placed heraldry showing the marriages between the Pympes and three prominent local families.[81] If a suitable lineage did not exist, it could be confected. In his will of 1523, the Kentish gentleman Reynold Peckham asked for a stone to be placed on his tomb depicting him with a wife and children, even though he died a childless bachelor.[82] Lineage and property were intimately connected. The nobility's estates were usually acquired through marriage or inheritance as large, coherent blocks of land. The family from whom these lands were acquired was remembered through the maintenance of their religious patronage and the preservation of their titles, and this memory could be useful in substantiating claims to disputed property, and also enhanced the prestige of the new owners.[83]

3

THE DISSOLUTION OF MARRIAGE
AND ITS CONSEQUENCES

Annulment and Separation

All of the canonical impediments to marriage could render a marriage invalid, resulting in annulment, or release 'from the bond of marriage' (*a vinculo matrimonio*), but not all necessarily did so. While impediments such as incest, pre-contract and pre-existing vows of chastity automatically invalidated a marriage, impediments of force or error could be overcome if the couple subsequently consented to the marriage. Christ had declared the sole grounds of divorce to be the wife's adultery.[1] The medieval Church abided by this teaching, but provided that under certain circumstances a married couple could live separately without breaking the marriage bond, an arrangement known as a separation 'from bed and board' (*a mensa et thoro*). This was available in cases of adultery, religious offences such as blasphemy, heresy or apostasy, and serious physical abuse. This last did not usually apply to anything short of life-threatening violence suffered by the wife, since husbands were allowed to use physical force to 'correct' their wives. Couples separated in this way were not free to remarry, and sexual relations with a third party constituted adultery.[2]

Whatever the original intentions behind the formulation of wide-ranging impediments to marriage, by the later Middle Ages at least, they do not appear to have been used as an easy means of securing an annulment. The records of church courts contain far fewer suits for annulment than suits for the enforcement of marriage contracts. Admittedly, this may be partly because many couples or individuals separated without taking their case to a court. We can never know the incidence of this 'self-divorce', but it may have been a widespread practice among the lower orders. Also, an unquantifiable number of suits alleging pre-contract may have been contrived in order to end a perfectly valid marriage of which one or both spouses had grown weary. However, the likelihood is that most people took at least the four-degree rule seriously, and did try to marry outside these prohibited relationships. The later medieval Church does not appear to have offered kinship, or any other impediment, as a convenient escape route for failing marriages. Strict rules of evidence operated in its courts, where the presumption was always in favour of preserving settled marriages if at all possible: 'the Church courts were not divorce mills', in the words of Professor Helmholz. Proving a relationship beyond the first or second degrees was often difficult: to establish kinship at four degrees – back to a common great-great-grandparent – presented obvious problems, and not everyone was able to emulate a successful suitor in a York annulment case who was able to produce witnesses in their sixties, seventies, eighties and even one who was supposed to be 100 years old![3]

The bishop's court was not the only refuge for those who wished for an annulment. The Pope could provide dispensations for the annulment of marriage. Papal dispensations could only be secured after much expenditure: agents had to be hired at the papal curia, bribes had to be paid and messengers sent, so only the wealthy could consider this option. The cost could run into three figures, and threaten to eat up even quite sizeable gentry or mercantile estates. Nor was there any guarantee of success. While the fact that recourse to the papal curia was deemed necessary suggests that the suitor would not expect success before his bishop's consistory court, the papacy does not seem simply to have sold dispensations to those who could find the asking price. Dispensations were usually granted on condition that the local bishop's court would first establish that the claims made in the petition were genuine.[4]

However, there are cases where annulments do seem to have been procured in order to meet the needs of family aggrandizement. In 1344 a papal dispensation was granted to annul the marriage between Richard, Earl of Arundel, and Isabella, daughter of Hugh le Despenser. The stated grounds were that the couple had been children at the time of their betrothal, which had been brought about 'not by mutual consent, but by fear of their relatives'. The inconvenient matter of their son (in fact there were three children) was explained away as being the product of a forced union. The annulment was granted, and within the year Richard had married Eleanor, daughter of Henry, Earl of Lancaster. The question of consent was not the crucial factor here. Richard's first marriage had allied his family with Edward II's favourite, but it had been devalued by the Despensers' downfall, and so he cast aside Isabella for the daughter of the current royal favourite. Infertility might also render a wife burdensome. In 1313 John de Warenne, Earl of Surrey, sought an annulment from his wife, Joan of Bar, on the grounds of consanguinity, despite a papal dispensation having been granted for this impediment at the time of the marriage seven years earlier. There had been no children by the marriage, whereas John had produced children by his mistress, Matilda de Neyrford. This attempt proving unsuccessful, he then tried to claim pre-contract with Matilda, but was again thwarted. The most famous divorce in English history, Henry VIII's from Catherine of Aragon, was of course provoked by the couple's inability to produce a son; had Pope Clement VII not been under the thumb of Catherine's nephew, the Emperor Charles V, Henry might have got his annulment. Even among the elite, the number of such cynical marital suits was always tiny, but it may be that the nobility and royalty had a more cavalier attitude towards the termination of marriage. There were of course higher stakes to play for, and their exalted positions and close relations with the princes of the Church may have tempered their awe of ecclesiastical institutions and their workings.[5]

Pleas for separation from bed and board (*a mensa et thoro*) did not come before church courts with great frequency, perhaps because many couples simply agreed privately to separate; since the court's decision in favour of separation did not dissolve the marriage, leaving the parties free to remarry, there would often have been no reason to seek a formal judgement. The great majority of cases alleged the husband's cruelty as the grounds for separation. Some of the testimony makes harrowing reading. In York in 1410, a wife alleged that her husband cut her face so badly that her eye fell out onto her cheek, so that her mother had to replace it 'gently and subtly'. When ecclesiastical judges ruled on such matters, they generally tried to reconcile the couple if at all possible, operating, in the words of Helmholz, as 'a rather heavy-handed marriage counsellor'. A common expedient was to require the husband to promise to treat his wife reasonably in future, guaranteeing his good behaviour by finding sureties, pledging goods or money, or taking a solemn oath. Such conditions could be imposed even in instances of extreme violence, such as a York case of 1395/6 when a wife alleged that her knife-wielding husband chased her into the street, stabbed her in the arm and broke one of her bones; on the other hand, 20 years earlier an allegation that a husband had thrown a knife at his wife gave sufficient grounds for the same court to grant a separation. Rather than simple judicial inconsistency, Helmholz prefers to interpret these decisions as evidence that ecclesiastical judges took a broad view of the circumstances surrounding the allegations, basing their judgements on their estimation of the couples' chances of salvaging some kind of working relationship from the wreckage of marital violence.[6]

Where separation was granted, there is some evidence that husbands might be required to pay alimony. In the Rochester consistory court in 1439 one man was ordered to make annual payments of 26s. 8d. to his wife.[7] Such provisions could also be made as part of an agreement with the spouse. In 1301 one Hertfordshire villein who was about to separate from his wife granted her a house and land on condition that she did not come near his own house, and that if she tried to prevent the separation she would lose everything.[8] In the event of an annulment, the wife's dowry was returned to her, unless she had been found guilty of adultery, in which case it was retained by her husband.[9]

Widows and Widowers

Marriages were brought to an end either by the couple's separation or by the death of one of the spouses. The latter was by far the commonest end, and it was much more likely to have been the husband who died first. For all ranks, the death of the head of household brought into being a new set of relationships. Widows assumed new freedoms and responsibilities, or remarried into a new family; children inherited property, were transferred into another's custody, or married – sometimes all three; while more distant kin might find their fortunes transformed by inheriting part of the deceased's estate. Death brought transition, and the end of one nuclear family often cleared the way for the birth of another.

Widows were common in medieval society. In 1436, 13 out of 52 peerage estates were held jointly between male heirs and dowager widows, while five were held outright by dowagers. Perhaps as many as two-thirds of noblemen and gentry left widows, half of whom may have lived another 16 years after their husbands' demise. On manors before the Black Death between 8 and 18 per cent of the tenancies may have been held by widows. Between 70 and 80 per cent of male rural testators left widows, as did 53 per cent of the male testators whose wills were proved before the London Hustings Court between 1258 and 1500. In later medieval towns, perhaps as many as a quarter of households may have been headed by widows. In early Tudor Coventry, there were nearly nine times as many widows as widowers.[10]

So many men left widows because wives tended to be slightly younger than their husbands, and on average probably lived longer, despite the perils of repeated childbirth. The proportion of widows in the total population is also determined by the length of time widows remained in that state before either remarriage or death. The incidence of remarriage was related to economics in terms both of the availability of alternatives to marriage and the financial attractions of the widow, but demographic, social and political pressures could also influence a widow's decision to remarry or remain single.

The death of her husband threw the widow into a new and challenging situation. Whatever grief she may have felt had to be put to one side as she attended to the demands of the moment. For most propertied widows, the two most pressing matters to be settled were her husband's business affairs and her own financial security. Many women were named as executors by their husbands. This might seem surprising, given the limited public profile which medieval society allowed married women. In fact, the large number of executor-widows is evidence that many women were one-half of a business partnership. The executor had to have a detailed knowledge of the testator's affairs, and in many cases there was no better candidate for this position than the widow. The implementation of her husband's will, the collection of debts and the provision of a tomb, charitable bequests and prayers could sometimes take years to complete.[11] The responsibilities of the executor could be burdensome, and also perilous. For some, widowhood brought the unwelcome attentions of their late husbands' creditors. One fifteenth-century Bristol widow, Joan Baten, named as executor by her husband, refused to act in this capacity because she knew that her husband's debts could not be satisfied from his estate. The property was therefore sequestered by the bishop of Worcester's commissioner and divided among the creditors. Meanwhile, Joan fled from her husband's house, supposedly taking with her only the clothes she stood up in, and took refuge in London, but to no avail, for she was sued in a London court by one of her husband's unsatisfied creditors. The refusal to act as executor, or denial of responsibility for their husbands' debts, was a common tactic among the widows of debt-ridden husbands.[12] A widow trying to distance herself from her husband's creditors needed to take care, for using any part of her husband's estate made her liable to be regarded as the administrator of his property, a role similar to that of executor, and therefore carrying responsibility for the payment of his debts. Such was the mistake made by another Bristol widow, Joan Keye. Her husband drowned at sea leaving great debts. After his drowning, but before she knew of his death, Joan used some of his property to discharge a number of his debts, and therefore became liable to be sued by his creditors.[13] Securing what was due to the widow by her dower, jointure, her husband's testamentary bequests and custom could be no less fraught with difficulty and danger.

The dower and jointure arrangements made at the time of her marriage were often not the entirety of a widow's entitlement. If she held land in her own right, as an heiress, this would revert back to her control on her husband's death. In addition, she might have received a proportion of his moveable goods, or chattels (some of which may originally have been hers anyway, since any goods she brought to the marriage became the property of her husband during his lifetime). At least in the twelfth and thirteenth centuries, the common law placed strict controls on the disposition of the husband's chattels after his death and the payment of his debts: if he left a widow and children, one-third would go to the former and one-third was to be divided among the latter; if there were no children, the widow would receive half. The share of chattels due to the widow was known as her *legitim*. The residue was expected to be used to finance the husband's religious and charitable bequests. However, legal opinion in the royal courts of later medieval England appears to have regarded what the testator did with his chattels as being none of its business, and it is likely that a fourteenth- or fifteenth-century widow would meet little success suing for her *legitim* there. She might have fared better in the ecclesiastical courts in northern England. The Church claimed that the testator's duty to employ a portion of his chattels for pious uses gave its courts the right of jurisdiction over *legitim*, and while the province of Canterbury appears not to have insisted on this right, the province of York continued to regulate the distribution of *legitim*.[14]

However, even when not legally bound to do so, many husbands left moveable property or cash to their widows, and in doing so generally seem to have followed the pattern prescribed by the old law of *legitim*. For the landed classes, such provision did not eat into the core of their wealth. If the widow took this moveable property out of the family by a second marriage, all that was lost was a non-renewable resource, unlike land which could continue to yield profits into infinity. Moreover, the husband may have considered it fitting that those domestic items with which his wife had been most concerned during their married lives should remain in her keeping. Even more appropriate was the return of items which the bride had brought to her marriage, and which under common law had thereby become her husband's property.[15]

For the urban widow, her husband's moveables would often have represented the bulk of his wealth. Perhaps for this reason, a form of *legitim* survived in London and, possibly, Bristol. Townswomen within the province of York would also have been able to sue for *legitim* in ecclesiastical courts.[16] Many urban widows would also have been entitled to freebench, the right to occupy all or part of her husband's principal dwelling. In London the custom of freebench also gave the widow a life interest in her husband's copyhold land and city rents, but she lost her freebench if she remarried. Probably, a London widow was not entitled to her dower while she enjoyed her freebench, but on marrying again she received her dower in compensation for the loss of freebench.[17] In later medieval Bristol, the widow's rights to her husband's freehold property were limited to two elements: freebench in her husband's principal tenement, and dower given at the church door, comprising named properties making up one-third of her husband's total holding at the time of marriage.[18] While the retention of *legitim* in towns certainly made sense in terms of securing the widow's interest, the continuance of nominated dower in later medieval Bristol suggests that these variations from common law were at least as much the product of local conservatism and inertia as concern for the fair treatment of women.

Nor were those who held by Kentish gavelkind tenure bound by the common law rules on dower and *legitim*. Gavelkind entitled the widow to one half of her husband's lands and one-third of his chattels, or a half if there were no surviving children, but only so long as she remained unmarried.[19] In many villages, widows' freebench consisted of one-half of their husbands' lands; this they could continue to hold if they remarried, but at their deaths it passed to their husbands' heirs. The conditional nature of a widow's possession of her freebench is suggested by the fact that freebench property could not be alienated without the heirs' consent. While many peasant widows benefited from their late husbands' arrangement of a form of jointure, whereby the lord settled the husband's land on the couple in joint survivorship, they might have been forced to relinquish all or part of the property when their sons were old enough to inherit. Peasant widows were usually left their husbands' principal tenement: of 235 widows of peasant testators, 63 per cent were bequeathed the main tenement for the duration of their lives. Many of these testators had underaged heirs, and so the major part of their holdings was available for the widow's support until the eldest son attained his majority. For the less-favoured remainder, provision varied from a room in the main house to the return of dowry or a dower of one-third of the property. Moveables were also frequently left to peasant widows. For the most part, peasant husbands' provision for their widows was generous, with many trying to go beyond the basic requirements of common law or custom.[20]

Where husband and wife held joint tenancies the widow did not need to pay an entry fine when she received her share in the holding, but she would still have to find the heriot, the surrender of the 'best beast' to the lord on the death of his tenant as a form of death duty, while the Church took the second-best beast as mortuary payment. The value of the heriot was assessed in relation to the value of the tenement, but was paid out of the deceased's chattels, as a reminder that, ultimately, these were owned by the lord, not by his tenant. During the later Middle Ages surrenders of livestock were increasingly commuted to cash payments, but these could still represent a considerable burden for peasant widows. Heriot was owed both by free and servile tenants, but the latter often had to face still more onerous exactions on the death of the head of the household. On several manors in Devon and Cornwall, for example, lords had the right to confiscate all of a villein tenant's chattels on his death. While, at least in the later Middle Ages, this right was rarely enforced to its full severity, the common practice of demanding a third of the chattels must often have had dire consequences for a villein widow. By the fifteenth century a considerable number of villeins were enjoying relative prosperity, and so became tempting targets for exploitative lords, particularly at moments of family crisis. After the death of her wealthy villein husband, Margery Heyne had to pay her lord £40 for permission to remain in her house and for the recovery of her moveable goods. When she remarried, her merchet, combined with a fine for entry into her previous husband's property, was set at £100, while her new husband was charged £40 to enter her lands.[21]

For most widows, from countesses to cottagers, it was land that provided the key to future security, transmitted either as dower or as jointure. Widows as young as nine could be eligible for dower, despite the canon law ruling that 12 was the earliest at which girls could be properly married.[22] The widow claiming her reasonable dower had to do so from her husband's heir, and this could sometimes lead to protracted disputes. Common law allowed the widow to stay in her husband's former principal residence for 40 days, assuming this to be a sufficient period in which she could secure her dower; after 40 days she had the right to a dower house, but not to live in the principal residence. In reality, the process of claiming dower from the heir could take far longer: after the death of Richard, Earl of Gloucester, in July 1262, it took his widow, Matilda de Lacy, over six months to receive her dower, but even then it was still contested by her son, while in 1411/12 Margaret, widow of John, Lord Darcy, had to wait almost a year for hers.[23]

What was promised to the bride by her marriage settlement was not always delivered when she became a widow. Enfeoffments to use, combined with the last will and testament, provided landholders with considerable freedom in the disposition of their property. This freedom could at times be used to circumvent the provisions of a marriage settlement. For example, in his will of 1494 William Brent, a Kentish gentleman, instructed the feoffees of all his lands to hold them to the use of his widow Anne, but when his son and heir John came of age, they were to convey the property to him, with the condition that he pay an annuity to his mother.[24] From that point, the annuity would replace Anne's jointure. The annuity had definite advantages for the heir, since it allowed him as an adult to enjoy all of his inheritance, rather than having to share it with his mother, subject only to a regular cash payment. In addition, if his mother remarried it did not put any of the family estates at the mercy of her second husband, who might be tempted to asset-strip the property during her lifetime in the knowledge that he would lose it on her death: William appreciated this, since he provided for his widow's control of the jointure to be replaced by an annuity in the event of her remarriage before his son came of age. Such were the advantages of the annuity – from the husband's point of view – that the wife was sometimes persuaded to accept an annuity rather than jointure lands from the very beginning of her widowhood. In such cases, the payment could be made conditional on the widow never attempting to claim her jointure lands. Needless to say, the widow often found the annuity less satisfactory, since it put her at the mercy of the party from whom she received her payment. In this, however, she was not necessarily any different from the widow whose jointure lands were held to her use by feoffees, who could exert significant control over her.[25]

Widows of husbands who held their lands by the free tenures of knight service, socage or serjeanty, that is, everything other than villein tenure, could plead for the allocation of their dower before the royal courts, and dower was the only major civil plea that required the woman to be the plaintiff, rather than have a man plead on her behalf. However, only the poorest plaintiffs would have had to plead in their own person, since for those that could afford his services, an experienced attorney was a far safer option. Nevertheless, the records of widows' pleas for dower suggest that many of these women had a good knowledge both of the law and of their husbands' property. In London, widows are found suing for their dower in the city courts, with varying degrees of success: of those who sued for their dower before the London court of common pleas, just over half were successful.[26]

The defendants in dower suits were often sons or stepsons. A variety of defences could be mounted against a widow's suit, including the claim that the marriage had been invalid, that the husband had not held by free tenure, or even that he was not actually dead. In addition, since the common law required that a marriage had to have been celebrated at church door before dower could be assigned, what may have been regarded by the Church as a valid marriage may not have been sufficient for a successful dower suit, as one thirteenth-century widow discovered to her cost. The man whose mistress she had been for many years lay dangerously ill, and in fear for his soul he married her with a ring and vows of present consent; the banns were read, but no solemnization took place at church, and for this omission she was denied her dower.[27] Alternatively, the defendant could claim that the widow, during her husband's lifetime, had renounced her dower in return for some other benefit, leaving one to wonder how often wives were forced or tricked into swapping their dower lands for something less valuable or even worthless.[28]

The defendant might have claimed that the widow had committed adultery. Under the Second Statute of Westminster of 1285, a widow could still be entitled to her dower if her adultery had been forgiven by her husband. The usual way of demonstrating this forgiveness was by the husband allowing her to continue living with him. Therefore, a woman accused of adultery who was ejected from her home, or who voluntarily left to live with her lover, had little hope of dower. In 1300 William Paynel and his wife Margaret sued for Margaret's dower from her previous marriage to John de Camoys. Margaret had left John to live with William, and had not been reconciled to her first husband. Thus far, she had no case. But the couple then produced an extraordinary document, a deed which they claimed had been made by John, recording that he had voluntarily surrendered his wife and her chattels to her lover. Apparently, their claim that this deed cleared them of the charge of adultery had already been accepted by an ecclesiastical court, but the royal judges were not so generous, or gullible, and their suit was dismissed.[29]

One further threat to a widow's enjoyment of her dower might be presented by her husband's political activity. Quite apart from, in some cases, starting her widowhood with the sorry and gruesome task of petitioning the king to be allowed to remove her husband's head and quarters from public display so they could be given a decent burial, a traitor's widow might also have faced the prospect of losing her lands, since she could not claim dower from forfeited property, and her own inheritance, subsumed into her husband's, would have been at risk. Widows in this predicament had no other option than to trust in the mercy of the very king against whom their late husbands had rebelled. Philippa, widow of Robert de Vere, Earl of Oxford, had to throw herself on the king's mercy after the de Vere lands were forfeited in 1388; she was lucky, and was granted a lifetime annuity of 1000 marks in recognition that she was the king's cousin.[30] From 1388 jointure was protected from forfeiture, and during the Wars of the Roses this provided a lifeline for families who found themselves on the losing side.[31] In 1461 the forfeiture of the estates of Henry Percy, Earl of Northumberland, who had fought for the defeated Lancastrians, might have meant oblivion for this great northern family, had it not been for the jointures of two Percy dowagers, together worth almost £2000 per annum.[32] The jointure rights of the widows of those adjudged as traitors were not always respected. Sir George Brown of Surrey and Kent was executed for his part in Buckingham's Rebellion against Richard III in 1483. His forfeited lands were divided among Richard's supporters without parliamentary sanction, and the usual procedures to determine the rights of those who may have had a claim on his property were not followed, with the result that his widow, Elizabeth, was forced to sue for a pardon and the return of her jointure.[33]

Before the thirteenth century, the feudal lord could impose a heavy fine on his vassal's widow before allowing her to enter her dower, particularly if she had refused his chosen partner for her remarriage, and there are even cases of the lord succeeding in denying the widow any dower at all. The king was perhaps the worst offender, since having as his immediate vassals the realm's greatest landholders, he faced the greatest temptation and the least possibility of effective resistance. In his coronation charter of 1100, Henry I promised that widows of tenants-in-chief would not have to pay the Crown before being allowed their dower and inheritance, but this promise was not kept for long. John (1199–1216) was a particularly notorious royal extortionist. To give one example among many, Margaret, widow of Ralph de Summery, was made to pay 300 marks to have her reasonable dower.[34] This was one of the abuses tackled by Magna Carta in its revision of 1217. Women widowed after 1217 were not to be made to pay for their dower.[35] This did not remove all possibilities for royal meddling in widows' property entitlements. In the 1470s Edward IV (1461–83), in order to build up suitable landed estates for his two brothers, the Dukes of Clarence and Gloucester, and for his son, the Duke of York, illegally appropriated dower and jointure properties from the countesses of Warwick and Oxford and the duchess of Norfolk.[36]

In contrast to the uncertainty and extortions faced by widows of Anglo-Norman and Angevin England, by the later Middle Ages the gradual strengthening of the widow's position in common law and the widespread adoption of jointure had brought about what might almost be described as a 'golden age' for propertied widows, despite the occasional depradations of unscrupulous monarchs. While jointure property could be the sole source of income for a widow unable to claim dower, such unfortunates were in a minority, and many widows enjoyed both jointure and dower. This often gave the widow a substantial share of her former husband's property, and for what had been a particularly desirable match, this could amount to almost his entire estate. For a few magnate dowagers, widowhood brought immense wealth, particularly if they had survived several husbands. One of the wealthiest of fourteenth-century widows was Elizabeth de Burgh, three times widowed, who spent the last 40 years of her life as a dowager with an estate worth around £3000 per annum.[37]

Among the elite, the combination of youthful marriage, often with a significant age difference between husband and younger wife, and women's generally greater longevity, meant not only that many women experienced widowhood more than once, but also that some after the end of their final marriage had many years still ahead of them. Even more impressive than the 40-year widowhood of Elizabeth de Burgh are the records of some of the daughters of the Neville family, such as the 48 years during which Euphemia, daughter of Ralph Neville (d. 1367), was a dowager to the Clifford family, or the example of Margaret, daughter of Ralph, first Earl of Westmoreland, 43 years a Scrope dowager. In the words of K. B. McFarlane, 'Nevill ladies ... were monstrous tough.' Capping all of these was Marie de St Pol, 53 years a widow following the death of Aymer de Valence in 1324. Such women were prodigies, but even widows of far less durability could dash the hopes of heirs and condemn landed families to generations of obscurity, and sometimes even oblivion in the male line. The Clifford estates were shared with at least one dowager throughout the period from 1314 to 1436, making it difficult for that family to play its part in national and regional politics, while Rowena Archer has concluded that 'The relative obscurity of the Mowbray family from its first elevation to an earldom in 1377 to its extinction must in some way be attributed to a remarkable run of tough old mothers.' In 1435 the Fitzalan earldom of Arundel was burdened with no less than three dowagers. The early fifteenth-century Courtenay earls of Devon were wrong-footed by both a long-lived dowager and a long minority, allowing their rivals, another branch of the family – the Courtenays of Powderham Castle – and the Bonvilles, to establish themselves in their former sphere of influence, leading to widespread disorder in the South West. The presence of a robust dowager could cast a blight over an heir's marital prospects, and could cheat him out of the enjoyment of his complete inheritance altogether. Katherine Neville outlived three generations descended from her first marriage to the duke of Norfolk. Further down the social scale, Margaret Freville survived her husband, Sir Hugh Willoughby of Warwickshire, by nearly 50 years, outliving her son in the process.[38]

Even when dowagers did finally die, the lands they passed on to their heirs may not have been in the best condition. The widow enjoyed only a life interest in her dower and jointure lands. In cases where the heir was her own child, one might expect maternal feelings to persuade the dowager to keep her lands in good order, but this was not always the case. In 1376 Joan, widow of John de Mohun of Dunster, sold the remainder interest in his property to Elizabeth Luttrell. She was able to do this since John had enfeoffed his lands to her use seven years earlier. As a result, at her death her three children – all daughters – were left with nothing save the dowries they had already received. When the heir was a more distant relation, the temptation to squeeze the most out of the property, felling trees and neglecting essential maintenance, might have been irresistible. Elizabeth, widow of John, Lord Mowbray, had been unable to resist, at least according to the suit brought by her stepson in 1366. He was awarded damages of almost £1000, but he died soon after the judgement, leaving Elizabeth in control of her dower lands until 1375. That temptation would have been much harder to resist, or not resisted at all, by a second husband, who would have had control over her dower and jointure lands and often precious little sympathy for the future security of his stepchildren and their heirs.

Perhaps it is too easy to see later medieval dowagers from the expectant heir's point of view, as impediments to the smooth unfolding of patriarchal ambitions, awkward women who would not do the decent thing and through their early deaths leave the way open for the younger generation – preferably male – to enjoy the undivided inheritance. This is not the whole story. Where the heir was underage, a mature, experienced widow could sometimes keep his inheritance safe until his majority, and act as a trusty advisor thereafter. We can also see the wealth and security which some – by no means all – widows enjoyed as their due reward for years sacrificed to further the plans and ambitions of fathers and husbands, doing their duty by sublimating their own desires in order to provide cash, connections and heirs for their male kith and kin. Contemporaries may have been uneasy at the thought of powerful, independent women, we should not be.

Chaucer's Criseyde extolled the freedom given to her by widowhood:

> I am mine own woman, well at ease,
> I thank God, as after my estate
> ....
> Shall no husband say to me 'check mate'[39]

And, indeed, a noble dowager who had secured her lands, avoided remarriage and enjoyed reasonable health, could live in some style and with a considerable degree of independence. The household book of Alice de Bryene, widow of Guy, Lord Bryene, gives us a snapshot of

how one wealthy widow lived in 1412/13. The impression it creates is
of an active, confident woman, making her mark in county society,
entertaining her gentle neighbours on a lavish scale, and presiding
over a reasonably well-regulated, substantial household.[40] For other
wealthy widows, the nunnery was sometimes an attractive prospect. A
well-born, resourceful widow who entered the religious life could
reasonably expect to achieve a position of authority within the cloister
while maintaining a certain degree of influence in the world outside.
For example, Ela, the widowed Countess of Salisbury, founded Lacock
Abbey in Wiltshire in 1232, and was its abbess for 20 years. This was
always only an option for a small minority, and there were other ways
of serving God and staying single. Some arranged with a local nunnery
to stay as guests, but without entering holy orders. Widows could also
take vows of celibacy but remain in the world, thereby avoiding the
dislocation associated with taking the veil while at the same time
removing themselves from the pressure to remarry.[41]

In towns, the widows of prosperous burgesses usually continued to
enjoy a high standard of living. The widows of merchants and craftsmen
sometimes carried on their husbands' businesses, at least until the
existing apprentices had left or the son and heir was ready to take
over. The widow of a London or Exeter citizen inherited her husband's
freedom, and could become a member of his former guild. One of the
most notable of fifteenth-century urban widows was Alice Chestre of
Bristol. From soon after her husband's death in 1470 until her own in
1485, Alice traded in cloth, wine and iron with Wales, Flanders, Spain
and Portugal. From the profits she was able to build an impressive
three-storey house in the centre of Bristol. However, a far greater
number of urban widows ended their lives in poverty. In later medieval
towns, greater concentrations of single women are found living in the
poorer quarters, in back streets and suburbs outside the fashionable
areas. Many of these would have been widows. Half the widows of early
Tudor Coventry lived alone, many in dire poverty.[42]

Some peasant widows flourished, buying land and selling produce,
and were able to make arrangements to ensure the future prosperity
of themselves and their children. Peasant widows tended to be much
more active in the public life of their village than they had been as
wives, but they were still prevented from serving as manorial officers
or joining tithings, since it was assumed that men, not women, were
normally heads of household and held authority. Nevertheless, Bennett
believes that public reticence and humility were expected of peasant

wives and daughters because they were subjected to the authority of husbands and fathers, not because they were women *per se*, and therefore it was not breaching contemporary norms for a widow to assert herself in the public arena. The assertive, secure peasant widow was always in the minority, however, and many at the lower end of society would have ended their days as vagrants.[43] For some widows, prostitution may have seemed the only means of survival, and several cases of widows entertaining men who then murdered them suggest that these women were selling sexual favours.[44]

Moralists were suspicious of widows, particularly if young and attractive, since it was the common male opinion that, having tasted the fruit of sexual pleasure, they would be unable to live chastely, and so were likely to lead young men into temptation. Since the widow could not be expected to restrain her lust, remarriage might be the safest option. The Church was uncertain whether it was advisable for widows to marry again, but allowed that they could if they wished. Late Roman law had prevented widows from remarrying within a year of their husbands' deaths, but this restriction was finally removed by Pope Alexander III (1159–81).[45]

The attitudes of male testators to the prospect of their widows remarrying varied from downright prohibition, on pain of losing some or all of their property, to the provision of property to take to the second marriage. A husband might be troubled that his widow's remarriage would allow another man, quite possibly a complete stranger, the enjoyment of three things previously reserved to him alone: his wealth, control of his children and his wife's body. Widow remarriage, with some justification, was often seen as threatening the interests of heirs. On the other hand, he might accept the regrettable necessity for his wife to find another husband who, he hoped, could safeguard her interests and those of his children, who could work the family holding, maintain the family business along with their apprentices, or represent his wife in court, but this generous attitude is rarely voiced by testators. The ease of disposition provided by enfeoffment to use, and other sophisticated legal devices, meant that medieval propertied husbands could, if they wished, hold the threat of disendowment over their widows. Many widows had to make the choice between remarriage and the full share of the marital estate.[46]

Many widows were willing to exchange their freedom for the economic support, companionship and protection of another husband. The widow's chances of remarriage were strongly influenced by economics. With so many younger women around, generally considered more physically attractive, with more years ahead of them and unburdened by another man's children, the widow's selling point had to be her wealth. Remarriage was not usually an option for the poorer widow with little property.[47] In times of higher demand for land, such as the period before the Black Death, and in places where there were fewer opportunities to supplement agricultural income by such activities as industrial production, craft work or fishing, the landholding widow would find it easier to attract a husband. In one Cambridgeshire village in the late thirteenth and early fourteenth centuries, perhaps as many as 40 per cent of all marriages were to widows. On some manors a pattern has been observed of a wealthy peasant widow marrying a younger man, who retained a sizeable part of her property after her death, which he used to attract a younger second wife – who would in turn survive him to start the cycle once again. Propertied widows could demand generous marriage settlements. Among villeins this, combined with the high level of entry fines which lords charged to their second husbands, meant that only the wealthier peasants could contemplate marrying a relatively wealthy widow. Where agriculture was not the only source of income there would have been a different equation. Here, there was less incentive to acquire land through marriage. Demand for widows as marriage partners might therefore be lessened in pastoral, wood or marshland regions, where as few as one in 13 widows might remarry. After the Black Death, land could be acquired with relative ease through means other than marriage. Some peasant widows actually refused their deceased husband's lands after 1348 because they had little confidence in attracting either hired labour to work them or a second husband. In Halesowen, the remarriage rate for widows either side of the Black Death declined from at least 63 to perhaps as little as 26 per cent.[48]

In towns some widows could support themselves through employment in manufacturing or service industries, typically by working in textiles, brewing and retail. For those to whom employment gave economic security and independence, remarriage became a choice rather than a necessity. Thus, greater employment opportunities for women after 1348 may have reduced the number of widows seeking remarriage, since the alternatives were more attractive. However, many urban widows may have had little realistic prospect of remarriage. Most later medieval towns seem to have attracted greater numbers of female than male immigrants, leading to a significant imbalance between the sexes, and making hopeless many a widow's quest for a husband.[49] Economics was not the only factor in patterns of widow remarriage. Widows who employed live-in male labour may have found it necessary to marry in order to avoid the scandal of an unmarried woman sharing her house with one or more unmarried men. The chosen husband might even have been a trusted household servant. Urban widows sometimes married their late husband's senior apprentice, a situation which promoted continuity in the management of the family business. Some widows had problems obtaining the property left them, perhaps because their sons refused to release it, and in such cases they may have considered remarriage as a means of securing their inheritance. A second husband might have had more authority over employees and servants, and perhaps over his stepchildren, than his new wife, and he could represent her interests in the courts. Widows with young children might have been under particular pressure to marry again.[50]

The widows of prosperous merchants could often pick and choose among a number of suitors. In the fifteenth century George Cely, London merchant and Calais stapler, was one of several suitors for the hand of Margery, widow of fellow stapler Edmund Rygon. George won his prize, but in doing so he spent more than £485 on land for her dower as well as jewels, plate and expensive jewellery, and bore the cost of the wedding feast, a total expenditure which his sister-in-law claimed had consumed all the inheritance he had received from his brother. Another merchant was willing to spend £20 on a go-between who promised to persuade a wealthy London widow to marry him rather than her other suitors. For Isabel, widow of the wealthy Hull merchant John Green, a suitor's unwelcome attentions degenerated into writs of trespass and debt against her, to which she retaliated in kind. There was a strong tendency for urban widows to take second husbands from the same guild to which their first husband belonged. Those who survived two or more husbands could amass spectacular fortunes. The aptly named Thomasine Bonaventure started life as a shepherdess, and after surviving three husbands (one a mayor of London) she died a very wealthy widow.[51]

Some widows chose to marry younger men from a lower social stratum, perhaps from within their own household.[52] Not even the daughter or widow of a king was averse to marrying 'beneath her' when the opportunity arose. Joan of Acre, daughter of Edward I and Eleanor of Castile and widow of Gilbert de Clare, secretly married Sir Ralph de Monthermer, a Clare household officer described by one chronicler as 'elegant in appearance but poor in substance', while her father was negotiating her marriage with Amadeus of Savoy. When the news broke, Joan's reply to her furious father was reported as, 'it is no disgraceful thing for a great and mighty earl to marry a poor woman in a lawful union and so it was neither blameworthy nor impossible for a countess to advance a capable young man.'[53] Whether she said it or not, this is an astute comment, highlighting the double standard in attitudes towards the choice of marriage partners between men and women – marrying a woman from humbler stock might be regarded as unwise or eccentric, but not disgraceful – and also suggesting why – apart from the obvious – an older woman might want a younger man as her partner. A widow, faced with the management and protection of her estates, and with limited administrative experience, would be wise to marry a man of proven capabilities – a man, perhaps, whose skills she had been able to appreciate at first hand within her own household. She might also be loath to exchange the comparative freedom of widowhood for the all-too-familiar yoke of marriage to a senior, more independently powerful man, so here again, marriage to a younger, formerly dependent individual might have offered the chance of a more equal partnership. Such thoughts might well have been shared by Katherine de Valois, Queen-Dowager of Henry V, when she contracted a secret marriage with Owen ap Maredudd ap Tudur, probably a member of her household or estate staff. But, with both Joan and Katherine, we must not discount a more basic motivation: while we may be sceptical of a sixteenth-century story that Katherine first noticed Owen whilst he was swimming in a river and thereafter conducted a secret liaison disguised as her own maid, earlier tradition consistently describes her interest in him as being more than merely pragmatic.[54]

    Katherine was one of three fifteenth-century widows whose activities after the death of their first husbands influenced English political history. Among the children of Katherine and Owen was Edmund, Earl of Richmond, who in 1455 married Margaret, the 12-year old daughter of John Beaufort, Duke of Somerset. He made her pregnant within the year, 'his wish to secure a life interest in her estates taking priority over any concern for her safety and well-being', in the words of Jones and Underwood.[55] Their son was the future Henry VII (1485–1509), and Margaret's two subsequent marriages after Edmund's death in 1456, to Henry Stafford and Thomas Stanley, Earl of Derby, added to her existing Beaufort inheritance to give her a sufficient power base from which she could play a major part in bringing about her son's eventual succession, and she remained his steadfast and highly effective supporter throughout his reign.[56] The third example is Elizabeth Woodville, widow of Sir John Grey, who had died fighting on the Lancastrian side at the second battle of St Albans in 1461. She secretly married Edward IV (1461–83) three years later. The marriage, or at least the promotion of her relatives that followed, was one of the most important factors that led Richard Neville, Earl of Warwick, to rebel against Edward and throw in his lot with his erstwhile Lancastrian foes, thereby initiating another round in the Wars of the Roses.[57]

Around half of the widows of peers in the fifteenth century did not remarry. Perhaps they chose to remain widows because they had ample resources with which to sustain themselves as single women.[58] Of those noble widows who did remarry, some accumulated three, four or even more husbands. Katherine, daughter of Ralph Neville, was born around 1400, and married her first husband, John Mowbray, later Duke of Norfolk, in 1412. After his death in 1432 she married successively Sir Thomas Strangeways and John, Viscount Beaumont, and then, in 1465, Edward IV forced her to marry her fourth and final husband, the 20-year-old Sir John Woodville, the King's brother-in-law. This is how the match was described by one outraged chronicler: 'In the month of January, Catherine, Duchess of Norfolk, a slip of a girl of about eighty years old [sic], was married to John Wydeville, the queen's brother, aged twenty years; a diabolical marriage ...'. And she outlived him by 14 years![59] Joan, granddaughter and heiress of John, Lord Cobham, had even more husbands. She had married her first by 1380, and she had two more between 1391 and 1407. Her fourth was Sir John Oldcastle, the Lollard leader executed in 1417. Her fifth, and final, husband, Sir John Harpenden, was still alive at her death in 1434. By the end of their lives, such much-married widows were presented with difficult choices when it came to deciding with which husband they wished to be buried. Not all opted for the most prestigious, or the one with whom they had lived longest or had the most children; sometimes, one suspects, it was simply the husband with whom they had been happiest.[60]

The right of widows to choose their own marriage partner or to remain unmarried was established in canon law by the middle of the twelfth century. Henry I's coronation charter of 1100 promised that the widows of his tenants-in-chief would not be married off against their wills, suggesting that this had been the case under his predecessors, but the price for this freedom – a fine paid to the king – was sometimes too high for the widow to pay, making this an empty promise. Kings continued to be the most assiduous of feudal lords when it came to enforcing their rights over their vassals' marriages.[61] In 1199 the widow of Ralph de Cornhill had to pay King John (1199–1216) 200 marks, three horses and two goshawks in order not to marry Godfrey de Louvain and to have the freedom to marry whom she wished. In 1318 Isabella, widow of John de Hastings, had her dower lands confiscated after she had married Ralph de Monthermer against the king's will, and for their return Ralph had to pay a fine of 1000 marks, although he was later pardoned this sum. This couple were generously treated compared to Elizabeth, widow of Thomas Mowbray, who married against the king's will in 1399 and for this suffered the temporary confiscation of her dower and a fine of 2000 marks. Two other later medieval widows, Margaret, Lady Roos, and Katherine Neville, each had to pay around £1000 to placate royal disapproval at their marriages, while Sir Nicholas Thorley was imprisoned for marrying the dowager Countess of Oxford against the king's will. The king could sometimes use the threat of withholding a widow's dower to prevent her from marrying without his leave: in 1375 Anne, the widow of John, Earl of Pembroke, was only assigned her dower after she had taken an oath not to marry without royal licence.[62]

Kings welcomed the financial benefits of asserting their control over the marriages of their vassals' widows, but it was the opportunities this presented for patronage that were more important. A wealthy dowager was a choice plum with which the king could reward his most favoured servants. Edward II (1307–27) fully appreciated this. Two of his household knights received as their wives two sisters, Margaret and Elizabeth, who were not only heiresses to two-thirds of the Clare inheritance, but also dowagers: Margaret from her marriage to Piers Gaveston, Earl of Cornwall, and Elizabeth as widow of John de Burgh and Theobald de Verdun.[63]

Dowagers might be violently coerced into marriage. Cases of abduction and marriage are not unknown: in the 1320s Eleanor, widow of Hugh le Despenser, was abducted and married by William de la Zouche, and despite the claim that she was already married, she continued as his wife. What was represented as an abduction might sometimes have been an elopement, with widow and future husband colluding in what was in effect an escape from a projected forced marriage. Such may have been the reality behind Theobald de Verdun's supposed abduction of Elizabeth de Burgh from Bristol Castle in 1316.

For some women, widowhood occupied a greater part of their adult life than marriage, and as such was perhaps the most significant part of their lives: it was widowhood that defined their personal identity.[64] They had no control over their entry into widowhood – the death of a husband, after all, was not something usually engineered by his wife – but once in this state many widows found themselves in positions of unaccustomed independence. For some, widowhood brought comfort and freedom; but these fortunates were probably in the minority. For many more, widowhood would have brought uncertainty, poverty, and no real increase in their freedom since they might be placed in a position where remarriage was unavoidable. For some, as we shall see, it meant the loss not just of a husband, but also the loss of custody over at least one of their children.

Entry into widowhood must often have been disorientating, with the widow's grief compounded by the burden of settling her husband's affairs and uncertainty about her future security. For most widowers, on the other hand, while the grief must often have been very real, the practical consequences of the loss of the spouse were less severe. Naturally, the widower continued to hold his own property, and his wife's business affairs would rarely have been as extensive as his own, so the demands of settling her affairs would have been correspondingly less. Only a small minority of married women made wills, since the moveable goods they had brought to the marriage became their husbands' property, and while they retained possession of their freehold land, this was under their husbands' control, so at least as far as the common law was concerned they had nothing to bequeath. Thus, unless he was one of the few husbands who had given his wife permission to make a will, the widower would not have a will to submit to probate and to execute. Neither would he have to worry about losing custody of his children, since this had always been vested in him, not in his wife. In addition, both the common law and most customary laws operated what was known as the 'courtesy of England', whereby a widower could hold for life any property his late wife had brought to the marriage, provided that there had been legitimate children. This applied even if their only child had lived just long enough for its cries to be heard by men who could testify to the fact in a court of law: since only the testimony of men was admissible in court and only women were normally present at childbirth, this meant that the child would need to have survived long enough to be carried out of the room in which its mother lay and into the presence of men. Through courtesy the widower of a deceased heiress or dowager might thereby have control for the rest of his life of a substantial part of his former wife's property, to the great frustration of her prospective heirs.[65]

Wardship

With life expectancy low by modern standards and with minorities lasting until 21 or later, heirs often did not reach adulthood before the death of their fathers. Minors constituted over half of the heirs to the estates of fifteenth-century male tenants-in-chief.[66] The care of fatherless children and the management of their affairs was therefore a recurring theme among medieval families.

When the fatherless child was heir to property, his or her management could turn from a burden to an opportunity. In the common law wardship of the property of a fatherless heir who held by knight service or serjeanty and was under age, together with his custody and the right to arrange his marriage, belonged to his immediate feudal overlord, irrespective of whether the child's mother or any other relatives were still alive. If the tenant had held lands of more than one lord, each lord had the wardship of 'his' lands, but the custody of the heir and the right to arrange his marriage went to the liege lord, that is, the lord whose ancestor had first granted land to the ancestor of the tenant. The original intention of feudal wardship was to support and protect the fatherless heir and his inheritance, but the opportunities for profit presented by the wardship of an unmarried heir to substantial property soon led to a situation in which the role of guardian was regarded as a right or gift rather than a duty, and the ward became a commodity to be bought and sold. The value of the heir lay both in his inheritance of lands, the profits of which would be enjoyed by his guardian, who would have to account for his management of them only when the heir came of age, and in his person, for he could be married to a relative of his guardian, or his marriage could be sold on to a third party. The king enjoyed a prerogative right of wardship over his tenants-in-chief, which meant that no matter how much land the tenant held of another lord, if he held anything directly of the Crown, his heir was liable to become a royal ward. Since virtually all the great landowners were tenants-in-chief, this gave the Crown a very lucrative hold over the nobility, as well as many more humble. From the twelfth century the Crown operated what was virtually a market in the marriages of its wards.[67]

In the later Middle Ages the employment of enfeoffments to use could circumvent a lord's right to the wardship of the lands of his tenant's underage heir. The common law regarded the tenancy of land enfeoffed to use as vesting in the feoffees, not in the person to whose use the land was enfeoffed. Therefore, when that person died, his heir was not by common law heir to the enfeoffed land, and so the lord from whom the land was held had no rights of wardship over him. The careless or complaisant lord could find that his tenants had enfeoffed to uses all of their land, and so deprived him of valuable feudal incidents. While attempting to enforce their own feudal rights, tenants-in-chief were at the same time trying to evade the prerogative rights of their royal lord. In this, they were often successful, despite the Crown's theoretical ability to defend its prerogative rights against its tenants through a system of licensing their enfeoffments. The Crown required that a royal licence be secured before any lands held in chief could be enfeoffed, and so any attempt by a tenant-in-chief to evade Crown wardship through enfeoffing all his lands held in chief could, in theory, be forestalled by the simple expedient of refusing a licence.

When efficiently managed, the system allowed the king to keep control over his immediate tenants and provided a source of income, since licences were only granted for a price, and sometimes this could be substantial. However, kings from Edward III (1327–77) to Henry VI (1422–61) appear not to have been vigilant in the protection of their feudal incidents, and were perhaps reluctant to risk alienating powerful supporters for the sake of occasional windfalls. There may also have been an element of bowing to the inevitable in this, an attitude perhaps increasingly shared by the tenants-in-chief from the later fourteenth century, but the more important factor is probably these kings' preference for parliamentary taxation as a source of revenue. While not necessarily any more popular than feudal dues, the income from a grant of taxation was more predictable, and large sums could be raised in a relatively short space of time. Perhaps by easing prerogative exactions the Crown secured the parliamentary classes' acquiescence in the growth of taxation. The attempts by tenants-in-chief to insist on their rights to wardship seem largely to have petered out during the fifteenth century, although there were exceptions: mesne tenants who died suddenly before they could enfeoff their lands, or were simply negligent, could still leave their patrimony liable to wardship. To the extent that this was a battle lost, tenants-in-chief could view their defeat with a certain degree of equanimity. Since all landholders below the king were also tenants of another in the feudal pyramid, the erosion of feudal rights, while causing a loss of revenue from the wardship and marriage of a tenant's heir, did free the lord from the fear that his own heir might be placed at the mercy of a guardian who may have had no previous connection with the family, nor indeed any sympathy with the family's interests. Only the king stood to lose out completely, since he was nobody's tenant and – ultimately – everybody's lord. After a long period during which the royal prerogative of wardship was not rigorously applied, Edward IV (1461–83) began to enforce it more consistently, perhaps because he felt unable to insist on adequate grants of parliamentary taxation, and his lead was followed by Henry VII (1485–1509). Early Tudor England saw something like an arms race between Crown and tenants-in-chief, with lawyers on both sides devising increasingly sophisticated stratagems in their attempts either to evade or to enforce the Crown's prerogative rights of wardship.[68]

The king might adopt a rigorous policy on the evasion of wardship by his tenants-in-chief, but for its implementation he was dependent on local royal officials. Here was a weak spot, for these officials were themselves often tenants-in-chief, and so deeply ambiguous about the measures they were charged to enforce. Those whose interests were threatened by the prerogative were on occasion able to exploit these officials' laxity or mendacity to slip the noose of royal wardship.[69] For example, the Sussex esquire Robert Poynings had enfeoffed all of his lands held in chief before going off to his death at the second battle of St Albans in 1461, and felt able to commit to his wife Elizabeth the wardship of his underage son and heir, Edward; likewise, in his will of 1471, Sir Thomas Cobham confidently entrusted his underage heir to the care of his wife.[70]

The custody of a royal ward's person and lands, and his marriage, were usually sold to a third party. Sometimes they might be given as a reward for conspicuous service. The purchaser might be the ward's mother, if she had the necessary cash and the inclination. In any case, between the father's death and the ward's sale to a guardian, the child was probably left in the care of his mother. Indeed, in many cases the child remained with the mother even after the sale, with the guardian paying towards his charge's maintenance until a marriage was arranged; only then would the mother be required to relinquish her child, who would usually be taken to live with his future in-laws. Thus, many guardians never had actual possession of their wards, and some might have never even met them.[71]

Potential guardians might be willing to expend considerable time and money in acquiring royal wardships. As early as 1130, royal wards and their marriages were being sold for as much as 1000 marks. In 1423 Ralph, Earl of Westmoreland, paid 3000 marks for the wardship of Richard, the future Duke of York, and undertook to spend 200 marks per annum on his maintenance.[72] Further down the social hierarchy, in 1479 Sir George Brown was asked to use his influence with the king to help Edmund Paston acquire a wardship 'though it cost 4 or 5 marks the suit' – this money was intended for favours and inducements simply to obtain the right to buy the wardship.[73] Just how sought after such commodities could be is suggested by the wardship purchased in 1483 by Richard Feldyng, a London merchant, and his associates. The ward was Richard Warre, son of a Somerset esquire, who would enter his majority in 1491. For the custody of his inheritance and the right to arrange his marriage the Feldyng syndicate paid 200 marks, which meant that in order to make a financial profit on the deal they had to make over £16 per annum from the eight years left of his minority.[74] Courtiers and other royal servants were particularly well-placed to learn about new wardships coming within the Crown's gift, and they probably received a disproportionate share of the grants. Between 1486 and 1506 Sir Richard Guildford, Henry VII's Controller of the Household, received three wardships, including that of Elizabeth, daughter and heiress of Sir Robert Mortimer of Cambridgeshire, whom he married to his second son George, thereby allying himself with the Howard dukes of Norfolk.[75]

The experience of Elizabeth Mortimer highlights another benefit that accompanied the wardship of a propertied heir. Control over the ward's marriage could bring advantageous family connections that far outweighed the immediate financial return from the estates. Given high child mortality rates, the wise guardian married off his heir as quickly as possible. In 1433 Sir John Radcliff was granted the wardship and marriage of Elizabeth, daughter and sole heiress of Walter, Lord Fitzwalter, and Sir John immediately arranged for her to marry his son and heir: both Elizabeth and her betrothed were aged about three years old.[76] A guardian did not always seek to marry one of his own children to his ward, sometimes because the ward's family was not of sufficient standing, and sometimes because he wanted to offer the marriage to another family he wished to reward or with whom he sought to strengthen his connections. But marriages between wards – or former wards – and their guardians' children were common. The initiative did not always come from the guardian. At some time before 1488 Edmund Martyn, the grandson of Judge John Martyn, having just attained his majority, complained to his former guardian, John Alfegh, that the latter had 'never tended him any marriage'; in response, Alfegh offered his own daughter, and Martyn, 'considering that the said John Alfegh had married his mother, was the gladder to do him pleasure and was agreeable with that he would be his god father'.[77]

The buying and selling of wardships and marriages, and the removal of children from their mothers' custody with little apparent consideration for the psychological effect this could have on them, might well strike us as callous, and, in the words of Gairdner, as an 'evil system of bargaining in flesh and blood'. One might expect some contemporaries to have concurred, particularly those who had themselves suffered wardship. Such a one in the fifteenth century was Stephen Scrope, whose stepfather, Sir John Fastolf, sold his wardship for 500 marks when he was about 12 years old, 'through the which sale', Scrope later wrote, 'I took sickness that kept me a thirteen or fourteen years ensuing; whereby I am disfigured in my person and shall be whilst I live.' After three years Fastolf bought his wardship back again, judging that Gascoigne's intended marriage partner would not be to the boy's advantage. Scrope's verdict on his treatment by Fastolf echoes Gairdner's abhorrence: 'He bought me and sold me as a beast, against all right and law, to mine hurt more than 1000 marks', but Scrope also recorded, with cold nonchalance, how 'for very need, I was fain to sell a little daughter I have for much less than I should have done by possibility.'[78] Scrope was far from unique. Mothers might on occasion buy back their children from royal wardship, only to sell them again to the highest bidder.[79]

From the thirteenth century there were legal safeguards against wards being disparaged through marriage to persons clearly beneath them in the social hierarchy, and it was possible for a ward to refuse his guardian's proposed marriage partner, but this was at the price of paying the equivalent sum to that which the guardian would have received for selling his marriage. If the ward married on his own initiative, without his guardian's consent, he had to pay double the value to the guardian. In 1318 Thomas Wake, the former ward of Piers Gaveston, gave Edward II £1000 to be pardoned for having refused the marriage offered him and for then marrying without royal licence.[80] Male wards left their guardian's control on attaining their majority.

For females, release only came with their marriage, and so guardians were sometimes tempted to keep their female wards unmarried so that they might continue to enjoy their lands indefinitely. In 1275 the Statute of Westminster provided that the guardian would lose his right to his female ward's marriage if he had not married her off by her sixteenth birthday. This still left the possibility of putting her into a nunnery, thereby keeping her permanently single without infringing the provisions of the Statute. Such was the plan of Thomas of Woodstock. He married Eleanor, one of the two daughters and heiresses of the recently deceased Humphrey de Bohun, Earl of Hereford and Essex (d. 1373), and prepared her sister Mary to take the veil so that he could enjoy the Bohun inheritance undivided. However, while he was away in France his scheme was foiled by his brother, John of Gaunt, who seized Mary and married her to his son, the future Henry IV (1399–1413).[81] Another ward in imminent danger of claustration took matters into her own hands. Saher, Earl of Winchester, ordered Maud, one of his wards, to be despatched to a convent so that he could have her inheritance. En route, she met and seduced one John of Marston, whom she then persuaded to marry her![82]

Only the heir was liable to feudal wardship, and so fatherless children who were not in line to inherit lands held by the military tenures were left to the care of their friends and relatives. There were therefore two classes of wardship: one was imposed on heirs, and the other, and much more common, was freely arranged by the child's family. Fathers often willed that their widows should have custody of underage children, as one early Tudor testator put it, 'that my wife have a tender and a faithful love and favour in bringing up of her children and mine, as she will answer to God and me'.[83] Mothers were not the universal choice. In some circumstances it may have been felt that a single woman would be less able to protect her children's interests. The widow could remarry, in which case her loyalties might be torn between the children of her first and second marriages, or her new husband might mistreat her first husband's children. Consequently, some fathers shared the responsibility between their widow and their trusted friends, or even gave her no part in the protection of her children.[84] Manorial custom usually provided that in default of the mother, a fatherless child should be given into the guardianship of the mother's nearest male relative. This would usually be her brother, and the significance of the maternal uncle in medieval society is suggested by the existence of a Middle English word, eme, to describe this relative. The maternal uncle would not normally stand to inherit if the child died, but could be expected to have some kind of emotional attachment to his niece or nephew.[85] Most legal opinion warned against entrusting an heir to the mercies of a kinsman who would inherit in the event of the child's death. The notorious record of royal paternal uncles suggests the wisdom of this advice: Richard III (1483–85) probably had his nephews killed in order to establish himself on the throne, while John (1199–1216) had his nephew Arthur murdered in 1203. In both cases, removal of a brother's son opened the way for the uncle to inherit.[86]

The guardian was in a position of trust which could easily be abused. There was no expectation that guardians would accept the responsibility out of pure altruism, and so a reasonable degree of profiteering was allowed for, but the line between this and malpractice could easily be overstepped, and so arrangements were often made for guardians to render account for their management of the child and the inheritance at the end of their guardianship. Despite such precautions, abuses were frequent and sometimes resulted in litigation. The same Edmund Martyn who had agreed to marry his former guardian's daughter later alleged that his guardian had illegally taken £50 per annum from the Martyn manor of Graveny during his guardianship.[87] The damage that long wardships could inflict on family fortunes is illustrated by the example of the Frechevilles in fifteenth-century Derbyshire. Their patrimony was held in wardship under the Crown for about 30 years. The head of the family before this period had been a knight; after it, the highest office the Frechevilles could aspire to was tax collector.[88]

A wardship could be a valuable commodity, which some were tempted to acquire by overt theft. Tales told in medieval courts of law should be treated with caution, since incidents were regularly misrepresented, or even invented, but tales of abducted wards recur with sufficient frequency to suggest that this was a real problem. According to Margaret Hylpe's petition to the court of Chancery, brought between 1510 and 1515, she had been abducted from the custody of her uncle by a gentleman called Roger Harlakynden, who held her against her will for nine years, during which time he took the profits from her inheritance. Another Chancery case concerns the Sussex knight, Sir John Culpeper. Sir John married Agnes, the widow of Richard Wakehurst and the sister of John and William Gainsford. At his request, the wardship and marriage of Margaret and Elizabeth, the two daughters of Agnes by her previous husband, were conveyed to him; he 'promised on the faith and truth of his body, and as he was a gentleman', that he would not marry them off without first obtaining the approval of Richard Wakehurst's feoffees, who included Agnes's brothers. Sir John failed to keep his promise in a most spectacular fashion, at least according to the Wakehurst feoffees: he led a gang to Agnes's house, from where he forcibly removed the Wakehurst sisters and carried them to London. Some time after this they were married to Sir John's brothers, Richard and Nicholas Culpeper. The Wakehursts and Gainsfords refused to hand over the title deeds of the sisters' inheritances, indicating that they believed this outrage to have been prompted by the lure of their estates rather than by stirrings in Culpeper hearts. Eventually the dispute was settled, and some kind of understanding reached between the families: when he made his will in 1516, Richard Culpeper asked for prayers to be said for his parents-in-law, perhaps as a final gesture of reconciliation.[89] Katherine Vaughn, daughter of a Bristol merchant, was a veritable bartered bride if we are to believe the Chancery petition of William Coke, a merchant of Coventry. He claimed that he had contracted a marriage with Katherine, but before this could be solemnized her guardians took her away. Her uncle, Christopher Matthew, offered to secure her delivery to Coke in return for £20. Coke gave him the money, but after Matthew had persuaded Katherine's guardians to let him take her he did not deliver her to Coke, but instead took her to Wales, with the intention of marrying her to someone else, in return for £40. Undaunted, Coke offered Matthew more money – he claimed to have expended £140 on this sorry adventure – and eventually recovered Katherine.[90]

As well as those too young to defend their own interests, there were those who were incapable of fending for themselves through some mental condition. Such unfortunates were described as 'idiots', and were committed to wardship in the same way as the fatherless young. The prospects for the younger brother of an idiot heir must often have been bleak, with his father's lands in the hands of a guardian who could anticipate enjoying the revenue for the entire lifetime of the ward.

The fate of children whose parent or parents had abandoned them rested with neighbours, lords, or manorial courts. A child with a known history, and still better with a worthwhile inheritance, could probably be found a home without too much difficulty. Babies left bundled up on doorsteps or in church porches were a different matter, and in the absence of foundling hospitals or adequate ecclesiastical charity, their future survival might depend upon the humane impulses of whoever

happened upon them.[91] Some orphans were lucky enough to be
adopted by families with the means to give them a good start in life. In
her will of 1525 Katherine Chiche of Canterbury left 12 ewes and a
cow to John Farrer, by then a London apprentice, whom she had
'brought up in youth'. Sir Edward and Isabel Poynings of Sussex and
Kent brought up two foundling girls; in his will Sir Edward left £4 for
the dowry of one, found unchristened, and for the other, Mary, he
arranged an annuity of £4 until she married or became a nun, at which
point she was to have 200 marks.[92]

Inheritance

The tenure of property in medieval England was divided into two
fundamental categories, free and unfree. The free tenures, comprising
the two 'military tenures' of knight's service and serjeanty, and socage,
were, in theory, held by people of free status and from the twelfth
century were regulated under common law. The unfree tenures, in
theory held by the unfree, or villeins, were regulated by a variety of
manorial customs. The equation between freehold and unfree tenure
and personal freedom or servitude became less meaningful into the
later Middle Ages as inheritance and a developing property market
meant that a freeman might hold lands of both free and unfree tenures.
Different tenures had different inheritance customs, although from
its formulation in the twelfth century until the end of our period,
common law slowly but steadily extended its influence into customary
law as part of a process that would eventually lead to its emergence as
the universal law of inheritance in England and Wales.

The fiefs given by William the Conqueror to his vassals were not
intended to be heritable. Instead, they were held in return for service
and at the death of the tenant returned to the lord. However, within a
century of the Conquest the principle of heredity had triumphed. From
its first formulation in the twelfth century, the common law stated that
freehold land was to descend according to primogeniture among sons
– in other words, to the eldest surviving son – or, in the absence of
sons, it was to be divided equally among the daughters. By so doing, it
recognized a principle that had gradually been gaining ground among
freeholders in most of England over the previous 200 years. In Anglo-
Saxon England partition of estates among sons or daughters – partible
inheritance – was the usual practice. Primogeniture had only been

common in Normandy for about a generation before 1066, and it took a little over a century after the Conquest for it to be adopted as the usual pattern for freeholders in England. The equal partitioning of the inheritance among daughters seems to have replaced the practice of making the eldest daughter sole heir as recently as the 1130s, probably as the result of royal initiative. Primogeniture is essentially inequitable, and the curbing of younger sons' aspirations that it entailed was acceptable because the system suited the needs of the Anglo-Norman lords. Primogeniture, along with other systems of unigeniture whereby all or most of the property was inherited by one person, ensured that the holding remained largely intact as it passed from tenant to tenant. This had the advantage that an unfragmented holding was more likely to provide continuity in the services owed by the tenant to his lord, and in an age of castles it proved particularly desirable, since these could not be divided in the way that lands could. While the principle of equal shares among daughters in the absence of sons might be thought to have brought about exactly that fragmentation of the holding that primogeniture was designed to avoid, this was not entirely the case, since common law provided that the father's castle, like any hereditary office or title he had held, would descend to the eldest daughter. The distribution of the rest of his property between his daughters created a number of heiresses, and therefore increased other fathers' chances of finding a propertied bride for their sons – particularly their younger sons. The greater abundance of heiresses of tenants-in-chief also increased the king's income and reserves of patronage, since he could sell the marriages of those heiresses who were his wards.[93]

Primogeniture may also have been a reaction to increasing pressure on landed resources. For Anglo-Saxon landowners, the Conquest had meant the confiscation of property on a catastrophic scale. The redistribution of their land among the conquerors provided the latter with an unparalleled bonanza of acquisition. For about a century afterwards land was cheaply and easily available. Freeholders in the first century of Anglo-Norman England did not need to be bound by the harsh requirements of primogeniture. In the newly conquered territory, there was an abundance of confiscated land with which younger sons could be endowed. From the mid-twelfth century, as the supply of land began to slacken, it became more expensive for fathers to acquire land to provide for all of their children (or at least, all of their sons). In these more straitened circumstances, many may have had little option but to conserve the core patrimony in the hands of a single heir.[94]

Under the system of common law primogeniture, lineal descent was preferred over collateral, so that only if there were no surviving children, grandchildren, great-grandchildren, or other direct lineal descendants, would the heir be looked for among brothers, sisters or other collateral kin. Local customary law sometimes differed. Borough English operated as a system of ultimogeniture, whereby the youngest son of the first marriage inherited. The custom of Borough English was found fairly widely dispersed throughout England, but was particularly common on the Somerset levels, in the Essex marshes, and the East Anglian fens. The rationale behind Borough English was that older siblings could be provided for, during the father's working lifetime, with dowries, apprenticeships or a share in the holding, leaving the youngest son with the main tenement to inherit, but often along with the duty of caring for an elderly parent. The custom predates the Conquest, and originally it may have suited a situation where new land was being cleared and colonized, since it encouraged older siblings to establish themselves elsewhere. In cases where the father died before his youngest son reached maturity, the boy's elder brother might act as his guardian. Borough English may have resulted in earlier marriages for heirs.

Other local systems departed from either of these varieties of unigeniture, and operated on the basis of partible inheritance. Kentish gavelkind – a form of socage tenure – was one such partible inheritance regime, whereby the inheritance was divided equally among the sons or, failing male issue, among the daughters. Partible inheritance was also found in East Anglia, but was rare outside these areas. The custom may have been the remnant of more general practices expunged by the seigneurial preference for unigeniture, and surviving in pockets where manorial feudalism was weakest, or it may have had its origins in the customs of those Germanic tribes that settled the eastern fringe of southern England. Whatever the origins of partible inheritance, both Kent and the counties of East Anglia had extensive woodlands, marsh and fen which offered a range of non-agricultural activities to offset the most obvious disadvantage of partible inheritance – the subdivision of plots into unviably small units – by allowing income from these holdings to be supplemented from industry and craft. Non-partible systems of unigeniture inheritance tend to have been characteristic of open-field or 'champion' agricultural areas, found most typically in the Midlands, and associated with the most developed forms of manorial feudalism.[95]

Most manorial customs allowed for the distribution of some of the deceased tenant's chattels among his widow and children. Some of his goods would have been retained within the tenement for the use of the next tenant: this would usually include essential agricultural equipment, known as the 'heirlooms', from the Old English word loom, meaning any tool or piece of equipment. The heir was usually excluded from any further distribution of chattels. The remainder was commonly divided into three parts, one for the widow, one for the daughter(s) and non-inheriting son(s), and the third to provide for the deceased's bequests. Children might receive their share of the chattels before their father's death, either as dowry or to provide for their future in other ways, such as an education or apprenticeship. Daughters who took their dowries might then be disqualified from inheriting anything further if they had siblings who had not been similarly provided for.[96]

The rights of heirs were carefully safeguarded in both common law and manorial custom. There were strict rules about what land could be alienated, that is, permanently granted away or sold off, and in what circumstances this could be done. On many manors tenants could not lease their land for longer than their own lives, or for the lifetime of the lessee; even where permanent alienation was allowed, the heir had to have given his consent. Common law gave the heir the right of veto over the alienation of any part of his inheritance or deathbed grants of property which he would otherwise inherit, the latter provision designed to curb the undue influence of priests attending a landowner's final moments. Under the common law principle of *retrait lignager* kin were given first refusal on any land to be alienated; a similar stricture is part of many manorial customs. Dower or freebench was also inalienable without the widow's consent.[97]

However, property holders and tenants at all levels of society were not necessarily bound by these rules in making provision for their offspring. Even villeins showed considerable freedom and initiative in arranging the disposal of their property, and were on occasion able to sidestep customary law in the interests of providing for their kinfolk, despite their theoretical inability to make wills and alienate property. For the peasantry, there were several legal instruments available with which the constraints of custom could be circumvented. One was the surrender of property to the lord and its reconveyance back to the tenant and the person to whom he wished it to remain after his death, to hold jointly. Alternatively, the peasant could have a transfer of property witnessed by the manor court and entered on the court roll. Finally, wills were increasingly popular among the wealthier peasants, both bond and free, from the fourteenth century onwards. Generally speaking, customary rules of inheritance were only explicitly invoked when a peasant died intestate or without some form of settlement made during his lifetime. Most of those who had anything to leave took care to avoid this eventuality. Settlements could be made before the father's death, or he could retire, giving control of the holding to his son in return for support. In such cases, the heir's acquisition of his inheritance was a gradual process, whose early stages could be supervised by his father. Even in those areas where customs of unigeniture prevailed, few non-inheriting sons and daughters would have been left with nothing, and many could look forward to a share in the family livestock, farming or domestic equipment, cash, or even some purchased land. Failing this, non-inheriting children would be entitled to accommodation on the family tenement. The inheriting son might also help his siblings by providing them with portions of land or dowries.[98]

While few non-inheriting sons were left empty handed, they would have found themselves occupying a lower socioeconomic niche than their fathers unless they came into an inheritance at a later date. Partible inheritance provided what at first sight seems a much fairer distribution of property, but this was at the risk of breaking up holdings into uneconomically small units, a situation that benefited neither lord nor tenant. In practice, it is likely that such an outcome could usually be avoided or ameliorated, so that the incidence of unviably small plots was probably not much greater in partible areas than elsewhere. Only a minority of families produced more than two sons, so for the most part no more than a bipartite division was necessary. In addition, a joint heir might sell out to his brother or brothers, or the heirs might agree that only one should actually work the land, with suitable compensation being arranged. The active land market in Kent and East Anglia – itself partly brought into being by the exigencies of partible inheritance – often allowed small holdings to be increased by purchase so that they became viable economic units. In addition, the availability in these areas of alternative sources of income would sometimes have allowed for a decent living to be had even where the holding was in itself insufficient. Most peasants in areas of partible inheritance seem to have been prepared to live with the custom, but

Borough English became increasingly unpopular during the later Middle Ages and had been largely replaced by primogeniture by the fifteenth century. Generally, the priority for manorial tenants and their lords was to preserve holdings as economically viable units, preferably kept within the immediate circle of close relatives to ensure stability, and local customs were liable to be adapted or ignored if they conflicted with these imperatives, so that the inheritance patterns in unigeniture and partible inheritance areas were often very similar. This pragmatic approach was reflected in attitudes towards the illegitimate children of peasant tenants. These were unlikely to be considered as heirs if legitimate children survived, but if not, a bastard son might be allowed to occupy the tenancy for his life, the holding then remaining to the rightful legitimate heirs of his father.[99]

Customary controls were particularly weak after the Black Death. Land was now relatively cheap and plentiful, and this, combined with continuing high mortality rates, brought about a more rapid turnover in landholding and a more vibrant property market. Young people need no longer have awaited their parents' retirement or death before acquiring land. Children of the wealthier peasantry were often provided with small holdings which their parents had purchased for the purpose, while others could save enough to buy land for themselves. In these circumstances the strict inheritance order imposed by local custom had even less bearing on the actual behaviour of the peasantry. Peasant heads of families might react in different ways to this situation. The greater opportunities on offer elsewhere, and the desire to keep the heir on the tenement by making it worth his while to stay, prompted some fathers to operate a rigorous policy of unigeniture inheritance, promising all to one son and leaving non-inheriting offspring to make their fortunes elsewhere. The heir's enhanced expectations might then have constituted a sufficient incentive to remain under his father's authority. On the other hand, some heirs might have taken their chances elsewhere, while hoping that whatever their disappointed fathers might will, the manorial community's preference for heirs by blood over more distant kin or purchasers might none the less allow them to return to claim the family holding after their father's death.[100]

In deciding who should be allowed to inherit villein land, manorial courts often showed a preference for those who could establish a long-standing connection with the village through residence and blood relationship. They were often preferred over those more closely related to the previous tenant but by marriage only, or who had not lived in

the village. Lords might charge higher entry fines to tenants who had
not acquired the land through marriage or inheritance from a blood
relative, and such newcomers probably found it more difficult to
assimilate into village society and to maintain their claim, particularly
if it was contested by a kinsman of the previous holder.[101]

The common law had developed to meet the needs of the land-
owning elite, but in formulating rules of inheritance, the lawyers'
preference for simple, easily understood principles had produced a
system which, if followed to the letter, would have gone far beyond
what most landowners actually wanted to do. Most did not want to
leave their younger sons landless, and a good many also wanted to do
more for their daughters than the common law allowed. Among the
elite, ways had always been found to provide for younger sons. The
greater Anglo-Norman lords could simply carve out fiefs for their
younger sons or younger brothers, who would then become their vassals.
This practice of subinfeudation in favour of non-inheriting kin was
widespread: in 1166, 61 out of 140 barons had enfeoffed at least one
relative in this way. Whatever generous feelings fathers and elder
brothers may have had for their junior kin, their maintenance made
sense as a strategy for family survival, providing, in the words of
Professor Holt, 'a second team in case the senior line failed'. For the
most part, younger sons of the Anglo-Norman baronage were not, like
some of their French cousins, thrown out into the world with little to
live by but their fighting skills. Idealized as knights errant in chivalric
romance, these rootless adventurers were in reality often no better
than bandits. The relative stability of Anglo-Norman society, compared
to France, may have owed something to its more generous provision
for younger sons. In 1290 the statute of *Quia Emptores* prohibited
subinfeudation, but by then inflation and the increasing scarcity of
land had made this option impossible for all but the very wealthiest,
while the emergence of the enfeoffment to use had provided
landowners with a far more flexible means of distributing their
property.[102]

During the later Middle Ages the combination of the enfeoffment
to use, will and entail allowed landowners to determine the settlement
of their lands after their deaths. The landowner, having granted his
property to a group of feoffees who were to hold it to his use, could
then instruct them through his will that after his death they were to
deliver it to his chosen legatees, as a conditional grant. This had the
great advantage that the landowner could enjoy his properties

throughout his own life, knowing that after his death they would be apportioned as he wished rather than as common law or custom dictated. Younger sons in this period were at least as likely to enjoy a share of their parents' estate as their Anglo-Norman and Angevin forbears, but they were unlikely to have been bequeathed any of the family's core property, the patrimony that had been passed down through the generations. Typically, they would receive land which their fathers had purchased, sometimes specifically for this purpose, and this might be supplemented by bequests of money, moveables or other non-landed resources. In addition, they might also have a remainder interest in all or part of the patrimony if the eldest son died without legitimate children. In such a case, normally the next eldest brother would inherit, and so on until there were no more brothers. Those with remainder interests were in the hands of fate and biology. Naturally, the wealthier the family, the greater the chances of the younger sons being well provisioned. At the lower end of freeholding society, where there was only enough land to provide the eldest son with a viable estate, younger sons had to be content with other forms of provision, while wishing their elder brothers not too long or fertile a life. While the harsh imperatives of primogeniture were not followed to their extremity, most fathers were careful to preserve the patrimony in the hands of their eldest son.

A lucky handful of younger sons found fortune through marriage. The estate of a younger son would not attract an heiress whose wealth could bridge the gap between his fortune and that of his elder brother, but, given the high rates of mortality and infertility, a bride with apparently modest expectations could occasionally become an heiress to rolling acres. The vast majority, however, would always be poorer than their elder brothers, and younger sons of younger sons poorer still. That there could be younger sons of younger sons, in other words, that cadet branches could prosper, is thanks to the amelioration of primogeniture practised by most fathers. Younger sons, for the most part, were provided with the wherewithal to marry and have children of their own. This gentle 'molecular process of downward mobility' through the generations of cadets had important consequences for the character of English society.[103] Most landed families could find – if they so wished – relatives occupying far more humble niches in the socioeconomic hierarchy. Members of the same kin group regularly straddled the boundaries between noble, gentle and commoner.[104] So, English landed society could not develop a caste system. At the same time, the rarity of partible inheritance and the concern to preserve the patrimony ensured a high degree of stability: the kaleidoscope of wealth and status was not too rudely shaken with the turn of each generation.[105]

For all their employment of uses, wills, and other legal devices, medieval landowners could not behave as completely free agents. A profound sense of obligation to their lineage prevented many landowners, particularly in the upper reaches of landed society, from disposing of their property purely on the basis of personal preference. Ideally, the eldest son and heir, inheritor of the patrimony, would pass that patrimony, suitably enhanced, to his own son and heir, who would do the same for his, down through the centuries. This was an aspiration rarely achieved: the failure to produce male heirs saw to that. To have a more than even chance of producing a male heir who would survive his father, a couple had to produce four children. This was not easy, and about 40 per cent of fathers died without a surviving son and heir. Naturally, it was more difficult to produce a surviving heir in times of high mortality. Before the Black Death, about 72 per cent of male tenants-in-chief left sons or sons of sons; in the 50 years after 1348, this figure dropped to only 57 per cent. Cheated of a son, the landowner might look for another close male relative, such as a brother. Here too, the statistics tell a depressing story. Before the Black Death, only 14 per cent were succeeded by neither sons nor male collaterals – in other words, by a female heir – afterwards, the figure soared to 36.8 per cent. Only a dozen families of the peerage survived the fifteenth century by direct father to son succession, although at this, the most politically engaged, level, violent death in battle or by execution added greatly to the mortality rate. During the same century, 75 per cent of the families of East-Anglian testators failed to survive in the male line for more than three generations. Among a large sample of will-makers between 1430 and 1480, 54 per cent died without surviving children of either sex. Inheritance by females, bringing the male line to an end, could mean the disappearance of the family name (unless other branches of the family survived in the male line) and the fragmentation of the patrimony (if it was inherited by coheiresses who divided the patrimony between them). Later medieval landowners could not afford to be complacent about the survival of patrimony and family name, and contrived means to lessen the odds against family extinction.[106]

The use and the will gave landowners control over the next generation, but one further lifetime might not extend the lineage very far. The entail could allow landowners to extend their reach down many generations. The entail was a device whereby the enfeoffment of land was accompanied by restrictions on the categories of heirs to whom it could descend. To create an entail, the landowner granted his property to his feoffees who then granted it back to him under the new condition restricting its future heritability. This was often done as part of the marriage settlement. A grant in tail general could be inherited by women for want of appropriate male heirs, but property granted in tail male, as its name suggests, could only be inherited by a male. Each entail thus created a chain – or tail – of heirs. Of course, the effect of this was to restrict the freedom of action of the heirs to entailed land, and so what freedom landholders gained through the use they might lose through the entail. Individuals did try to break inconvenient entails, to the great profit of lawyers if not always themselves, but the landed classes in general accepted these restrictions for as long as they shared in the ideology of lineage that had given rise to the entail in the first place. In the words of J. P. Cooper:

... entails were all intended to exemplify the holding of property in common with those both born and unborn in the interests of a lineage and according to the more or less explicit directions of an ancestor, or the recognized customs of a family. What settlements of these kinds attempt is a stability and prolongation which mortality and other demographic factors deny to actual households.[107]

In view of the importance of lineage and the family name to landed society, it has usually been assumed that one of the main purposes of entails was to prevent the passing of the patrimony to female heirs, and with it the family name into oblivion. In the conditions of the later fourteenth and fifteenth centuries, when high levels of mortality brought the number of male heirs to unprecedentedly low levels, such an imperative should have been all the more pressing, so one would expect most entails to have been made in tail male. There are indeed famous examples of female heirs being excluded in this way. In 1349 Thomas, Lord Berkeley, entailed his patrimonial lands, including Berkeley Castle, in tail male, in a deliberate attempt to prevent their fragmentation among heiresses. Generations later, in 1417, this entail barred the heir general, Thomas's great-granddaughter Elizabeth, wife of Richard Beauchamp, Earl of Warwick, in favour of her cousin James Berkeley, and thereby provoked a family feud that lasted for half a century. However, in studying the property arrangements made by the peerage and other tenants-in-chief in the fourteenth and fifteenth centuries, Simon Payling has found that most noble families employed a combination of entails so that part of the inheritance would descend according to tail male, and part by tail general. Furthermore, entails in tail general tended to predominate, even to the extent that some families, their patrimony held in tail general, were unable to disinherit the female heir by this entail in favour of the more distant male heir, and so became extinct in the male line. This suggests that for many, concern for the future of all their children, not just sons, outweighed their desire to maintain the integrity of the patrimony and the survival of the family name. Quite simply, they could not countenance the disinheritance of a daughter in favour of more distant male kin, even at the risk of extinction in the male line. Combined with unusually high levels of mortality, this reluctance to create entails in tail male made the century or so after the Black Death in Payling's phrase, 'the last great age of the heiress'. Opinion may have been changing under the early Tudors, perhaps in reaction to the prevalence of wealthy heiresses and dowagers, and most of the examples of tail male being used deliberately to disinherit females come from this period. The 'age of the heiress' was also a time of considerable social fluidity. Heiresses provided a means whereby new blood – and, more to the point, new money – could enter the landed classes. Men who had made their fortunes in trade, military or administrative service, or in the law (perhaps drawing up entails, uses and wills for their future relatives) married their sons to landed heiresses, exchanging sordid cash for the social prestige of land and title.[108]

Not all fathers were as solicitous for their daughters' interests. For many, a suitable dowry was all they were prepared to give non-inheriting daughters. If there was no living son and heir, even unborn sons could be given precedence over their sisters. When the Kentish gentleman Richard Cressel made his will in 1508, he had only daughters and he left his lands to be divided equally between them, but on condition that they were to be disinherited if his pregnant wife produced a boy. His daughters must have awaited the birth of their sibling with unusual anticipation.[109]

The discretion that the use, will and entail gave to fathers could be used not only to benefit those children who could not otherwise hope to inherit, but also to disparage those who under common law or custom would have been the principal heirs. Parents might also have chosen to allocate more of their resources to the Church, putting their own spiritual welfare before the security of their children. Inevitably, there were tensions, both between parents and children and between siblings. Where different systems of inheritance operated simultaneously within the same family's holdings, the complications would have been compounded, and family relationships could thereby grow more than usually volatile. Such was the experience of the fifteenth-century Lovelace family of Kent. Richard Lovelace held three manors, two of which were held in gavelkind and the third divided into two halves, one held in gavelkind and the other in fee, according to common law primogeniture. These he entailed upon his eldest son and his daughter, disinheriting his two younger sons, who went on to prosecute their claims as heirs by gavelkind both in the courts and by violent direct action.[110]

One alternative to marriage for younger sons – as indeed, for daughters – was the Church. The popular view that children were often forced into holy orders because they were excess to the requirements of their family's matrimonial plans seems wide of the mark in most cases. While giving a child to the Church was usually cheaper than providing a marriage, it was not without its costs. Placing a son or daughter in a religious house required a gift, usually of land, and a son bound for the secular clergy needed at the very least a certain level of education and, preferably, a benefice, both of which cost money. A number of testators provided bequests to children if they should choose to take orders. In 1520,Roger Harlakynden willed that if his young son Alexander should wish to become a priest, he was to receive a £10 annuity which would pay for his education and that this would continue until he found a benefice worth £20 per annum. There is no hint of compulsion here, nor in many other similar examples. Even the ruthless William Haute and Richard Woodville stopped short of forcing Haute's daughter into a nunnery in their efforts to disinherit her in favour of any son by his second marriage.[111]

Illegitimate children were not unusual in landed society and were often provided for, whether or not they were openly acknowledged. Their acknowledgement was more likely when there were no surviving legitimate children. The only legitimate child of Sir Edward Poynings had died young, but he did have four illegitimate children. In his will of 1521, Sir Edward openly acknowledged their existence and took pains over their futures: his eldest illegitimate son was to receive all his purchased lands, his two younger sons were each to have remainder interests in this property and annuities, while his daughter was provided with a dowry of £40.[112]

Retirement

While most people did not survive much beyond their forties, perhaps 20 per cent lived at least into their fifties, when they would have been regarded as old by their contemporaries. At this age, their declining physical and mental powers began to make them a burden to the generations below them. Medieval moralists and poets stressed the duty that children owed to their aged parents. At the same time, there was a persistent fear of old age, which all too easily slipped from loathing of the condition to hatred of the person suffering from it, and the fact that admonitions to respect the elderly had to be repeated with such frequency suggests that many failed to do so. One can readily imagine the frustration of a son or daughter waiting to inherit from a parent who clung tenaciously to life.[113]

Elderly people generally tried to maintain their independence for as long as possible, but if death did not claim them first, the time would come when independence had to be surrendered. Manorial documents reveal frequent instances of retirement contracts, whereby an elderly individual granted his or her buildings and land to another – not necessarily a relative – in return for care. In some cases the lord arranged for an infirm tenant's holding to be worked by another who would undertake to provide care; the detailed arrangements were often left up to the village to decide. Presented with a tenant who could no longer work his holding effectively, it would have been in the lord's interest to encourage – or force – retirement, and in this he may well have been fulfilling the wishes of an impatient heir who could then take over the holding without having to wait for the tenant's death. Usually, however, the arrangements were made by the person retiring. For example, an ageing father could grant his son the use of his land, while reserving its control to himself, on condition that the son provided him with the necessities of life. There were also cases where peasant marriage settlements obliged sons or daughters-in-law to give support if their spouses predeceased their parents. Alternatively, arrangements could be made by a husband for the care of his widow after his death. Many retirement contracts contained clauses allowing for the carer to be replaced if that person did not provide the proper support, died or moved on. Some wealthier pensioners were able to retain separate accommodation, but most had to share their homes with the carer. Changes of personnel must have been distressing at times, particularly since there was something of a market in retirement contracts, carers selling out to others and moving on, so the person with whom the original contract was made may not have continued to care for the pensioner until death.[114]

Clark found that only one-third of pensioners had contracts with their own kin: this probably indicates that the majority of these did not have children living within the village, and were therefore dependent on others, who need not necessarily have been complete strangers. Sixty-four per cent of the contracts Clark used were made by single pensioners, suggesting that these were arrangements made by people at the very end of their lives who felt they could no longer cope alone. Many of these contracts come from the post-plague period, when land was relatively plentiful. The number of people willing to take on lands on the condition of providing care is at first sight surprising. Forty-four per cent of carers were married couples, 5 per cent single women and 51 per cent single men, suggesting that a majority were young people who had not yet inherited, or had little immediate prospect of inheriting, their parents' property and who saw this as an opportunity to establish themselves.[115] Such a suggestion raises questions about motive and the quality of care which might have been provided under this system. If the carers saw this merely as a foot up on the property ladder, would they have been sufficiently careful of their elderly charges? There were allegations of dreadful abuses. In Wakefield in 1286, the manor court heard how one carer evicted his pensioner and her son, killed her dog and stole her cloak and ten ells of her linen. Lacking surviving close kin, the elderly were dependent on the neighbours and the manor court to guarantee their rights. Their dependency would have been total if they were bedridden or suffering from dementia.[116]

The likelihood is that only a minority of the post-plague retirement contracts were made with the retiring person's children. Perhaps this is a reflection of the younger generation's increased propensity to leave home in search of better opportunities in an environment of low rents and high wages[117] Some of them may have found their first opportunity through entering into a retirement contract, undertaking to give to a stranger the care they had denied their own parents. Even where support agreements were made between retiring parents and their children, there was no absolute guarantee of good treatment. In essence, this is the arrangement made by Lear in Shakespeare's *King Lear*: he divides his kingdom between two of his daughters with the intention of living out his remaining years as their guest, but the evil Goneril and Regan turn their father out to wander on the moors. This story was current from at least the twelfth century, and, with the kingdom of Britain replaced by a tenement and a few acres, might have been repeated in any number of villages. While there may have been latter-day Gonerils and Regans in medieval England, the chances are that for many parents and children the arrangement was mutually beneficial: certainly, a number of sons contracted marriages soon after entering the land of their retired fathers.[118]

Alternatively, a caretaker or housekeeper could be hired to look after an ageing individual, but this solution required a considerable amount of surplus funds, and so would only have been open to the more prosperous peasant. Guilds could also provide some care to the elderly in town and country. In 1389 about a third of all guilds which submitted their charters to the Crown for inspection gave support to their members in sickness and old age. This might have entailed no more than a daily loaf of bread and help with funeral costs. More significant than their material benefits, perhaps, was the emotional support guilds provided, with their regular meetings, visits and prayers providing a kind of surrogate kin group for the otherwise lonely and isolated. Not every old person was caught in the safety nets provided by kin, contract and guild. Distressing tales of old people found frozen to death or drowned in wells and rivers while wandering in search of charity are to be found in the manor court rolls and coroners' records, indicating that a significant number of the elderly suffered desperate hardship.[119]

CONCLUSION

The household was the basic social and economic unit in pre-industrial society. The family provided the means whereby subsequent generations were created and socialized, and it was through kinship that property and status were transmitted. The family loomed large in experience and ideology.[1] Medieval constitutional theory owed a great deal to the ideology of the family: succession to the English throne was by primogeniture, and there was a strong feeling against the alienation of the royal patrimony.[2]

While there were casual unions and unmarried mothers in medieval England, the expectation, among those with property at least, was that families were created through marriage. Marriage gave men full membership of the community and determined the fortunes, and to some extent the identity, of women.[3] From peasants to the highest nobility, marriage was of fundamental importance in the redistribution of land. Without a legitimate son and heir, land might easily be lost from the male line or disappear from the family altogether.[4] Generally speaking, marriage practices and inheritance law and custom worked towards the survival of the patrimony in the senior line. The processes whereby non-inheriting children descended, and others rose through marriage to heirs and heiresses, have played a major part in rendering permeable the boundaries between socioeconomic strata: that English society has never evolved into a 'caste' system has much to do with the history of the family.

Marriage determined the fortunes of both individuals and families. With each union were created new alliances, new kin groups, and new property arrangements. Most of the medieval laity undoubtedly took marriage seriously. While we might cynically imagine that the wide net of kinship within which marriage was formally prohibited might have facilitated annulment and thereby engendered a cavalier attitude towards marriage, the records of church courts suggest otherwise.[5] Exact rates of illegitimacy are impossible to determine before the era of parish records and registration, but they are likely to have been relatively low, certainly by modern standards. However, this does not necessarily mean that couples waited until after the church blessing before having sex: probably, the common expectation was that betrothal sanctioned sexual relations, and many brides may have been pregnant when they appeared at the church door. The fact that there were not more unmarried mothers indicates that marriage was seen as a process rather than an event: in other words, the exchange of vows was, barring mishaps and deceit, the first in a series of steps that would lead, over a period of weeks or months, to the church blessing.[6]

The relationship between family and household structure and demography has occupied many historians. Attention has tended to focus on the later medieval period, when the survival of evidence makes large-scale statistical analysis possible for the first time. At what age, on average, did people marry for the first time? How many remained single? How long did the average marriage last? And how many children did the average couple produce? This last is the crucial question in judging the population's ability to maintain or increase its size in the next generation. As we have seen, there is no definitive answer to any of these issues, but a reasonable balance of probability on most. In particular, if proponents of a late marriage regime are correct, it would seem that patterns of nuptuality played a crucial role in holding back demographic recovery after the Black Death. Decisions to postpone marriage were probably linked to cultural expectations regarding household formation and the constraints imposed by economic opportunities, or the lack of them. If it was the case that most sons delayed marriage until they could establish separate households, and if a large proportion of adolescents of both sexes postponed marriage until after they had finished a period of employment, mainly as servants and apprentices, then the relationship between economics and family formation must be seen as crucial to explaining demographic trends in later medieval England.

With so many leaving home in their early teens, some never to return, the strength of attachment felt by medieval sons and daughters towards their parents must be questioned. We can never be sure of the relative importance of emotional bonds between the generations, between siblings, between spouses, and within wider kin groups; nor of how these were weighed in the balance against the bonds of friendship and neighbourliness. Such things are unquantifiable, directly at least, and are most susceptible to an infinite variety of individual predilections and circumstances. There is no doubt of the importance of the family in providing the framework within which most people led their lives; what is altogether more mysterious is the family's place in their hearts. While few historians have wholeheartedly endorsed Macfarlane's assertion that later medieval England was populated by rugged individualists for whom narrowly defined self-interest and market forces usually overrode loyalty or sentiment towards kinsfolk, his emphasis upon the individual does warn us against treating men, women and children in any age simply as numbers in a demographer's equation.[7] Historians have to generalize – and this book has necessarily been made up of generalizations – but in doing so they must always remember that what they are working with are the shadows left by real flesh and blood human beings. Those attempting to write the history of family relations, approaching the most private and intangible of human experiences, must especially remember this.

NOTES

Introduction

1. M. J. Levy and L. A. Fallers, 'The Family: Some Comparative Considerations', in B. Farber (ed.), *Kinship and Family Organisation* (New York, 1966), pp. 10–13.
2. L. Stone, *The Family, Sex and Marriage in England, 1500–1800* (London, 1977), pp. 20–30.
3. See in this volume, 'Marriage in Theory and Law', pp. 6–18; and, 'Inheritance', pp. 110–22.
4. For a recent and comprehensive summary of work on England's later medieval population and economy, see S. H. Rigby, *English Society in the Later Middle Ages: Class, Status and Gender* (Basingstoke, 1995), particularly pp. 60–103.
5. For an excellent introduction to the family in medieval Europe and beyond, see A. Burguière et al. (eds), *A History of the Family*, vol. 1 (Cambridge, 1996).
6. For early modern families, a good starting point is R. O'Day, *The Family and Family Relationships, 1500–1900: England, France and the United States of America* (Basingstoke, 1994).

1 Marriage Making

1. D. Herlihy, *Medieval Households* (Cambridge, MA, and London, 1985), pp. 6–10.
2. M. Foucault, *The History of Sexuality, Volume Three: The Care of the Self* (Harmondsworth, 1986), pp. 41–2, 80, 141, 167–85.
3. For the following paragraph, see P. Brown, *The Body and Society: Men, Women and Sexual Renunciation in Early Christianity* (London, 1990). J. A. Brundage, *Sex, Law, and Marriage in the Middle Ages* (Aldershot, 1993), pt ii, pp. 2–10; pt iii, pp. 195–7.
4. Genesis 2:24. All biblical references are to the Vulgate, the most widely used version of the Bible in medieval England: B. Fischer et al. (eds), *Biblia Sacra Iuxta Vulgatam Versionem*, 2 vols (Stuttgart, 1969).

5. Matthew 19:3–11; John 2:1–11.
6. Matthew, 10:35–7.
7. I Corinthians, 7:2–9; Ephesians, 5:22–33. C. Brooke, *The Medieval Idea of Marriage* (Oxford, 1989), pp. 48–50.
8. D. Herlihy, 'The Family and Religious Ideologies in Medieval Europe', in T. Hareven and A. Plakans (eds), *Family History at the Crossroads* (Princeton, NJ, 1987), p. 4; Brooke, *Medieval Idea of Marriage*, pp. 61–3.
9. Brundage, *Sex, Law, and Marriage in the Middle Ages*, pt ii, pp. 4–8.
10. Cited in P. J. Payer, *The Bridling of Desire: Views of Sex in the Later Middle Ages* (Toronto, 1993), p. 70.
11. Herlihy, *Medieval Households*, p. 11.
12. Ibid., pp. 48–51.
13. Brooke, *Medieval Idea of Marriage*, p. 58.
14. Ibid., p. 128; E. J. Carlson, *Marriage and the English Reformation* (Oxford, 1994), pp. 9–18; C. Morris, 'William I and the Church Courts', *English Historical Review*, 82 (1967), pp. 449–63; W. Seccombe, *Millennium of Family Change: Feudalism to Capitalism in North-Western Europe* (London, 1995), pp. 70–3; J. Goody, *The Development of the Family and Marriage in Europe* (Cambridge, 1983), pp. 148–50.
15. Carlson, *Marriage and the English Reformation*, p. 18.
16. G. Duby, *Love and Marriage in the Middle Ages* (Cambridge, 1994), pp. 16–7; M. M. Sheehan, *Marriage, Family and Law in Medieval Europe: Collected Studies* (Cardiff, 1996), pp. 126–8; Brooke, *Medieval Idea of Marriage*, p. 56.
17. Brooke, *Medieval Idea of Marriage*, pp. 63–87. G. Duby, *The Knight, the Lady and the Priest: The Making of Marriage in Medieval France* (Harmondsworth, 1983), pp. 116–20. For a succinct account of the 'Investiture Contest', see R. W. Southern, *The Making of the Middle Ages* (London, 1953), ch. 3.
18. For a representative sample of Georges Duby's work, in addition to *The Knight, the Lady and the Priest*, see *Medieval Marriage: Two Models from Twelfth-Century France* (Baltimore, MD, 1978); and *Love and Marriage in the Middle Ages*.
19. Herlihy, 'The Family and Religious Ideologies in Medieval Europe', p. 7, and *Medieval Households*, p. 86; Carlson, *Marriage and the English Reformation*, pp. 23, 25; Brooke, *Medieval Idea of Marriage*, p. 126.
20. Brooke, *Medieval Idea of Marriage*, pp. 128–32, 37–43. J. T. Noonan, 'The Power to Choose', *Viator*, 4 (1973), pp. 419–34; Sheehan, *Marriage, Family and Law in Medieval Europe*, pp. 84–5, 87–117, 121, 134–5, 160, 165–6, 173–6; C. Donahue, 'The Canon Law on the Formation of Marriage and Social Practice in the Later Middle Ages', *Journal of Family History*, 8 (1983), pp. 144–58; Herlihy, *Medieval Households*, pp. 9, 80–1; R. H. Helmholz, *Marriage Litigation in Medieval England* (Cambridge, 1974), pp. 25–65.
21. Sheehan, *Marriage, Family and Law in Medieval Europe*, p. 260; Carlson, *Marriage and the English Reformation*, pp. 23–5. See in this volume, 'Coercion and Freedom of Choice', pp. 23–31.
22. Helmholz, *Marriage Litigation in Medieval England*, pp. 60, 62–5, 90–4.

23. Ibid., pp. 98–9. Sheehan, *Marriage, Family and Law in Medieval Europe*, pp. 132–3.
24. Brooke, *Medieval Idea of Marriage*, p. 125.
25. Goody, *The Development of the Family and Marriage in Europe*, pp. 135–45; Herlihy, *Medieval Households*, pp. 6–7; Helmholz, *Marriage Litigation in Medieval England*, p. 78; Sheehan, *Marriage, Family and Law in Medieval Europe*, pp. 120.
26. Sheehan, *Marriage, Family and Law in Medieval Europe*, pp. 128–31, 254.
27. D. Herlihy, 'The Family and Religious Ideologies in Medieval Europe', in idem, *Women, Family and Society in Medieval Europe: Historical Essays, 1978–1991* (Providence, RI, and Oxford, 1995), pp. 163–4.
28. Helmholz, *Marriage Litigation in Medieval England*, p. 80.
29. Goody, *Development of the Family and Marriage in Europe*, pp. 145–6, 150.
30. Sheehan, *Marriage, Family and Law in Medieval Europe*, pp. 84, 253–6. Leviticus 18:6–18 prohibits sexual relations within two degrees.
31. Goody, *Development of the Family and Marriage in Europe*, pp. 34–47.
32. Sheehan, *Marriage, Family and Law in Medieval Europe*, pp. 247–61; Herlihy, *Medieval Households*, pp. 11–13.
33. Helmholz, *Marriage Litigation in Medieval England*, p. 89.
34. Sheehan, *Marriage, Family and Law in Medieval Europe*, p. 74; J. Murray, 'On the Origins and Role of "Wise Women" in Causes for Annulment on the Grounds of Male Impotence', *Journal of Medieval History*, 16 (1990), pp. 235–49.
35. Helmholz, *Marriage Litigation in Medieval England*, pp. 94–8.
36. D. Weinstein and R. N. Bell, *Saints and Society: The Two Worlds of Western Christendom, 1000–1700* (Chicago, IL, 1982).
37. Herlihy, 'The Family and Religious Ideologies in Medieval Europe', p. 5; Jacobus de Voragine, *The Golden Legend: Readings on the Saints*, trans. W. G. Ryan (Princeton, NJ, 1995), vol. 2, pp. 99–100, 221.
38. Voragine, *Golden Legend*, vol. 2, p. 304.
39. Herlihy, *Medieval Households*, pp. 118–20.
40. C. W. Atkinson, *The Oldest Vocation: Christian Motherhood in the Middle Ages* (Ithaca, NY, 1991), particularly pp. 101–43.
41. Herlihy, *Medieval Households*, pp. 127–9.
42. J. Hajnal, 'European Marriage Patterns in Perspective', in D. V. Glass and D. E. C. Eversley (eds), *Population in History: Essays in Historical Demography* (London, 1965), pp. 101–43; Hajnal made much use of J. C. Russell's analysis of the 1377 poll tax returns in his *British Medieval Population* (Alberquerque, NM, 1948), and T. H. Hollingsworth, 'A Demographic Study of the British Ducal Families', *Population Studies*, 11 (1957–8), pp. 4–26.
43. R. M. Smith, 'Hypothèses sur la nuptialité en Angleterre aux XIIIe–XIVe siècles', *Annales: Economies, Sociétés Civilisations*, 38 (1983), pp. 107–36, and 'Some Reflections on the Evidence for the Origins of the "European Marriage Pattern" in England', in C. Harris (ed.), *The Sociology of the Family: New Directions for Britain* (Keele, 1979), pp. 74–112. For a useful survey of the debate, see P. J. P. Goldberg, *Women, Work, and Life-Cycle in a Medieval Economy: Women in York and Yorkshire, c.1300–1520* (Oxford,

1992), pp. 204–15.
44. H. E. Hallam, 'Age at First Marriage and Age at Death in the Lincolnshire Fenland, 1252–1478', *Population Studies*, 39 (1985), pp. 55–69; C. Howell, *Land, Family and Inheritance in Transition: Kibworth Harcourt, 1280–1700* (Cambridge, 1983), pp. 222–5; B. Campbell, 'Population Pressure, Inheritance and the Land Market in a Fourteenth-Century Peasant Community', in R. M. Smith (ed.), *Land, Kinship and Life-Cycle* (Cambridge, 1984), pp. 128–9. L. R. Poos, *A Rural Society after the Black Death: Essex, 1350–1525* (Cambridge, 1991), pp. 129, 141; Goldberg, *Women, Work, and Life-Cycle in a Medieval Economy*, p. 232; C. Phythian-Adams, *Desolation of a City: Coventry and the Urban Crisis of the Late Middle Ages* (Cambridge, 1979), p. 84. See also Seccombe, *Millennium of Family Change*, pp. 152–6.
45. R. S. Gottfried, *Epidemic Disease in Fifteenth-Century England: The Medical Response and the Demographic Consequences* (New Brunswick, 1978), p. 177.
46. Z. Razi, *Life, Marriage and Death in a Medieval Parish: Economy, Society and Demography in Halesowen, 1270–1400* (Cambridge, 1980), particularly pp. 60–8, 131–7.
47. Goldberg, *Women, Work, and Life-Cycle in a Medieval Economy*, pp. 204–11.
48. Z. Razi, 'The Myth of the Immutable English Family', *Past and Present*, 140 (1993), pp. 3–44. However, Hanawalt's interpretation of the Suffolk poll taxes produces a picture similar to Razi's Halesowen: B. Hanawalt, *The Ties That Bound: Peasant Families in Medieval England* (Oxford, 1986), p. 96.
49. J. Ward (ed.), *Women of the English Nobility and Gentry, 1066–1500* (Manchester, 1995), pp. 21–2, citing Froissart's *Chronicle*.
50. M. Hicks, *Warwick the Kingmaker* (Oxford, 1998), p. 24.
51. K. Dockray, 'Why Did Fifteenth-Century English Gentry Marry?: The Pastons, Plumptons and Stonors Reconsidered', in M. Jones (ed.), *Gentry and Lesser Nobility in Late Medieval Europe* (Gloucester, 1986), pp. 65–6; A. S. Haskell, 'The Paston Women on Marriage in Fifteenth-Century England', *Viator*, 4 (1973), p. 466; *Complete Peerage*, vol. 3, pp. 346–7; J. G. Waller, 'The Lords of Cobham, Kent, Their Monuments, and the Church', *Archaeologia Cantiana*, 11 (1877), pp. 49–112; T. May, 'The Cobham Family in the Administration of England, 1200–1400', *Archaeologia Cantiana*, 82 (1967), pp. 1–31; S. M. Wright, *The Derbyshire Gentry in the Fifteenth Century*, Derbyshire Record Society, 8 (1983), p. 40.
52. Brooke, *Medieval Idea of Marriage*, pp. 152–7.
53. Stone, *Family, Sex and Marriage*, pp. 43–8; DuBoulay, *An Age of Ambition: English Society in the Late Middle Ages* (London, 1970), p. 100; Hollingsworth, 'Demographic study', pp. 4–26; Russell, *British Medieval Population*, pp. 156–8; Goldberg, *Women, Work, and Life-Cycle in a Medieval Economy*, pp. 223–4; Phythian-Adams, *Desolation of a City*, p. 84.
54. Based on data from the biographies of MPs in J. S. Roskell, L. Clark and C. Rawcliffe (eds), *The History of Parliament: The House of Commons, 1386–1421*, 4 vols (Stroud, 1992). Only those individuals for whom dates of birth and first marriage were known or could be estimated to within a few years were included in this sample.

55. Gottfried, *Epidemic Disease in Fifteenth-Century England*, pp. 181–3.
56. Helmholz, *Marriage Litigation in Medieval England*, p. 104; Wright, *Derbyshire Gentry*, pp. 40–1.
57. E.W. Ives, '"Agaynst taking awaye of women": The Inception and Operation of the Abduction Act of 1487', in E. W. Ives, R. J. Knecht and J. J. Scarisbrick (eds), *Wealth and Power in Tudor England: Essays Presented to S. T. Bindoff* (London, 1978), pp. 21–44; F. Bamford (ed.), *A Royalist's Notebook: The Commonplace Book of Sir John Oglander Kt. of Nunwell. Born 1585. Died 1655*, 2nd edn (New York, 1971), p. 235.
58. See in this volume, 'Coercion and Freedom of Choice', pp. 23–31.
59. P. J. P. Goldberg, '"For better, for worse": Marriage and Economic Opportunity for Women in Town and Country', in idem (ed.), *Woman is a Worthy Wight: Women in English Society, c.1200–1500* (Stroud, 1992), p. 120.
60. Goldberg, *Women, Work, and Life-Cycle in a Medieval Economy*, p. 231. But Gottfried did not find a strong correlation between wealth and age of first marriage in his analysis of fifteenth-century wills: *Epidemic Disease in Fifteenth-Century England*, pp. 164–75. Poos, *Rural Society after the Black Death*, pp. 131–2, 157–8.
61. Poos, *Rural Society after the Black Death*, pp.131–2, 162–70, 177–9; Razi, 'The Myth of the Immutable English Family', pp. 19–21, 33–42.
62. Goldberg, *Women, Work, and Life-Cycle in a Medieval Economy*, p. 232, and '"For better, for worse"', pp. 108–25; Seccombe, *Millennium of Family Change*, pp. 94–5, 156–9.
63. Cited in Poos, *Rural Society after the Black Death*, pp. 136–7.
64. Goldberg, *Women, Work, and Life-Cycle in a Medieval Economy*, pp. 243–4.
65. Poos, *A Rural Society after the Black Death*, p. 135.
66. Bennett, *Women in the Medieval English Countryside*, p. 95; Goldberg, '"For better, for worse"', p. 117; Hanawalt, *Ties That Bound*, p. 199.
67. Hanawalt, *Ties That Bound*, pp. 200–2; Smith, 'Some Reflections on the Evidence for the origins of the "European Marriage Pattern" in England', p. 97. Bennett found a similar high incidence of brides paying their own merchet, but in many cases without any evidence of prior economic independence: *Women in the Medieval English Countryside*, pp. 88–9.
68. Goldberg, *Women, Work, and Life-Cycle in a Medieval Economy*, p. 247.
69. Bennett, *Women in the Medieval English Countryside*, p. 96, and 'The Tie that Binds: Peasant Marriages and Families in Late Medieval England', *Journal of Interdisciplinary History*, 15 (1984), pp. 111–29; Hanawalt, *Ties That Bound*, p. 200.
70. Hanawalt, *Ties That Bound*, pp. 198–9.
71. Helmholz, *Marriage Litigation in Medieval England*, pp. 90–4.
72. The following is based on J. Gairdner (ed.), *The Paston Letters* (1983 edn, Gloucester), vol. 2, nos. 93–4; vol. 3, no. 374; vol. 4, nos 710, 713, 721, 842. C. Richmond, 'The Pastons Revisited: Marriage and the Family in Fifteenth-Century England', *Bulletin of the Institute of Historical Research*, 58 (1985), pp. 25–36, *The Paston Family in the Fifteenth Century: The First Phase* (Cambridge, 1990), pp. 178–81, and *The Paston Family in the Fifteenth Century: Fastolf's Will* (Cambridge, 1996), pp. 173–4, 205, 210–11.

Dockray, 'Why Did Fifteenth-Century English Gentry Marry?', pp. 71–4; Haskell, 'The Paston Women on Marriage in Fifteenth-Century England', pp. 459–69.

73. The same combination of family pressure and ecclesiastical insistence on the sanctity of the vow by present consent was apparent 300 years earlier in the case of Alice, the 12-year-old daughter of Henry, Earl of Essex. In 1163, soon after she had contracted marriage *per verba de presenti* with Aubrey de Vere, Earl of Oxford, her father fell from grace and she became worthless to Aubrey. He repudiated her, shutting her up in a tower in the hope that she would retract her vow, but a ruling from the papal curia forced him to accept her as his wife: Brooke, *Medieval Idea of Marriage*, pp. 152–7.

74. J. C. Holt, 'Feudal Society and the Family in Early Medieval England: The Heiress and the Alien', *Transactions of the Royal Historical Society*, 5th ser., 35 (1985), pp. 6–7, 23–4; S. Painter, 'The Family and the Feudal System in Twelfth-Century England', *Speculum*, 35 (1960), pp. 3, 8; E. Searle, 'Seigneurial Control of Women's Marriage: The Antecedents and Function of Merchet in England', *Past and Present*, 82 (1979), pp. 3–43; P. A. Brand, P. Hyams and R. Faith, 'Debate: Seigneurial Control of Women's Marriage', *Past and Present*, 99 (1983), pp. 123–48.

75. Sheehan, *Marriage, Family, and Law in Medieval Europe*, pp. 232–4, 242–6; S. L. Waugh, *The Lordship of England: Royal Wardships and Marriages in English Society and Politics, 1217–1327* (Princeton, NJ, 1988), pp. 52–63, 71–2, 87–90, 191–2, 207–8.

76. J. Scammell, 'Freedom and Marriage in Medieval England', *Economic History Review*, 2nd. ser., 27 (1974), pp. 523–37; and 'Wife-Rents and Merchet', *Economic History Review*, 2nd. ser., 29 (1976), pp. 487–90. E. Searle, 'Freedom and Marriage in Medieval England: An Alternative Hypothesis', *Economic History Review*, 2nd. ser., 29 (1976), pp. 482–6; Searle, 'Seigneurial Control of Women's Marriage', pp. 3–43; Smith, 'Some Reflections on the Evidence for the Origins of the "European Marriage Pattern" in England', pp. 96–7; Brand, Hyams and Faith, 'Debate: Seigneurial Control of Women's Marriage', pp. 123–48; E. Clark, 'The Decision to Marry in Thirteenth and Early Fourteenth-Century Norfolk', *Medieval Studies*, 49 (1987), pp. 496–516.

77. E. B. Fryde, *Peasants and Landlords in Later Medieval England* (Stroud, 1996), pp. 26, 176.

78. Smith, 'Some Reflections on the Evidence for the Origins of the "European Marriage Pattern" in England', pp. 96–7; C. Dyer, *Lords and Peasants in a Changing Society* (Cambridge, 1980), p. 366; J. A. Raftis, *Tenure and Mobility: Studies in the Social History of the Medieval English Village* (Toronto, 1964), pp. 129, 141–2, 179–82.

79. Searle, 'Seigneurial Control of Women's Marriage', p. 17.

80. Sheehan, *Marriage, Family, and Law in Medieval Europe*, p. 36; Raftis, *Tenure and Mobility*, pp. 40–1.

81. G. C. Homans, *English Villagers of the Thirteenth Century*, 2nd edn (New York, 1960), p. 188.

82. Seccombe, *Millennium of Family Change*, pp. 106–8; Carlson, *Marriage and*

the English Reformation, pp. 26–8.
83. Homans, *English Villagers of the Thirteenth Century*, p. 188.
84. C. Given-Wilson, *The English Nobility in the Late Middle Ages: The Fourteenth-Century Political Community* (London, 1987), pp. 42–4.
85. J. R. Lander, 'Marriage and Politics in the Fifteenth Century: The Nevilles and the Wydevilles'; in idem, *Crown and Nobility, 1450–1509* (London, 1976), pp. 94–126.
86. His acquisition did not go uncontested; for the full story, see Hicks, *Warwick the Kingmaker*, pp. 22–53.
87. A. J. Pollard, *North-Eastern England During the Wars of the Roses: Lay Society, War and Politics, 1450–1500* (Oxford, 1990), pp. 108–10; Wright, *Derbyshire Gentry*, pp. 46–9.
88. M. J. Bennett, *Community, Class and Careerism: Cheshire and Lancashire Society in the Age of Sir Gawain and the Green Knight* (Cambridge, 1983), pp. 26–30.
89. P. W. Fleming, 'The Character and Private Concerns of the Gentry of Kent, 1422–1509' (unpubl. University of Wales Ph.D. thesis, 1985), pp. 124–5, 457.
90. J. Kermode, *Medieval Merchants: York, Beverley and Hull in the Later Middle Ages* (Cambridge, 1998), pp. 80–1.
91. P[ublic] R[ecord] O[ffice] Early Chancery Proceedings C1/31/375.
92. J. C. Wedgwood, *History of Parliament: Biographies of the Members of the Commons House, 1439–1509* (London, 1936), pp. 216, 221.
93. E. W. Ives, *The Common Lawyers of Pre-Reformation England: Thomas Kebell: A Case Study* (Cambridge, 1983), pp. 383–8; Wedgwood, *History of Parliament*, pp. 656–7, 721.
94. P. W. Fleming, 'The Hautes and Their "Circle": Culture and the English Gentry', in D. Williams (ed.), *England in the Fifteenth Century: Proceedings of the 1986 Harlaxton Symposium* (Woodbridge, 1987), pp. 85–102.
95. C. Given-Wilson, *The Royal Household and the King's Affinity: Service, Politics and Finance in England*, 1360–1413 (London, 1986), pp. 217–8.
96. *Paston Letters*, vol. 1, p. 380.
97. S. Thrupp, *The Merchant Class of Medieval London* (Chicago, IL, 1948), pp. 256–68.
98. Wright, *Derbyshire Gentry*, pp. 27–8.
99. Dockray, 'Why Did Fifteenth-Century English Gentry Marry?', pp. 61–80; Richmond, 'The Pastons Revisited', pp. 25–36, for this and the rest of this paragraph.
100. C. L. Kingsford (ed.), *Stonor Letters and Papers, 1290–1483*, 1996 edn, ed. C. Carpenter (Cambridge), no. 123.
101. Ibid., no. 261.
102. Ibid., no. 166.
103. *Paston Letters*, vol. 5, nos. 897–8.
104. G. Chaucer, *The Canterbury Tales, The Merchant's Tale*, ll. 452–4.
105. S. Payling, 'The Politics of Family: Late Medieval Marriage Contracts', in R. H. Britnell and A. J. Pollard (eds), *The McFarlane Legacy: Studies in Late Medieval Politics and Society* (Stroud and New York, 1995), pp. 25–6.
106. Ibid., pp. 21–47; Wright, *Derbyshire Gentry*, pp. 32, 45–9.

107. R. H. Bremmer, 'Widows in Anglo-Saxon England', in J. Bremmer and L. van den Bosch (eds), *Between Poverty and the Pyre: Moments in the History of Widowhood* (London, 1995), pp. 59–61; R. E. Archer, '"Rich Old Ladies": The Problem of Late Medieval Dowagers', in A. J. Pollard (ed.), *Property and Politics: Essays in Later Medieval English History* (Gloucester, 1984), pp. 15–35, at 16; M. Mate, *Women in English Society* (Cambridge, 1999), pp. 17–18.

108. The following draws upon F. Pollock and F. W. Maitland, *The History of English Law Before the Time of Edward I*, vol. 2, 2nd edn (Cambridge, 1968), pp. 420–6, and Payling, 'Politics of Family' pp. 21–47.

109. K. B. McFarlane, *The Nobility of Later Medieval England* (Oxford, 1973), pp. 68–70; J. M. W. Bean, *The Decline of English Feudalism, 1215–1540* (Manchester, 1968), pp. 112–13, 220–34; T. F. T. Plucknett, *A Concise History of the Common Law* (London, 1956), p. 578.

110. W. S. Holdsworth, *A History of English Law*, vol. 3 (London, 1909), p. 196.

111. Plucknett, *Concise History of the Common Law*, pp. 551–2; Payling, 'Politics of Family' pp. 21–47.

112. S. Bentley (ed.), *Excerpta Historica or, Illustrations of English History* (London, 1831), p. 250.

113. Wright, *Derbyshire Gentry*, p. 31.

114. Payling, 'Politics of Family', pp. 35–7.

115. Homans, *English Villagers of the Thirteenth Century*, pp. 140–1, 161–2, 179–84; Hanawalt, *Ties That Bound*, p. 221; R. H. Hilton, *The English Peasantry in the Later Middle Ages* (Oxford, 1975), pp. 100–1.

116. Seccombe, *Millennium of Family Change*, pp. 105–6, criticizes Jack Goody's more upbeat assessment of the benefits of dowry in his *The Development of the Family and Marriage in Europe*, pp. 19, 232–9, 257.

117. Sheehan, *Marriage, Family, and Law in Medieval Europe*, pp. 118–61.

118. Helmholz, *Marriage Litigation in Medieval England*, pp. 25–65, 107.

119. Hanawalt, *Ties That Bound*, p. 204. Razi, *Life, Marriage and Death in a Medieval Parish*, pp. 152–3.

120. The following description is taken from Brooke, *Medieval Idea of Marriage*, pp. 248–9, and Homans, *English Villagers of the Thirteenth Century*, pp. 170–2.

121. Homans, *English Villagers of the Thirteenth Century*, p. 171.

122. Cited in Hanawalt, *Ties That Bound*, p. 203.

123. P. P. A. Biller, 'Marriage Patterns and Women's Lives: A Sketch of a Pastoral Geography', in Goldberg (ed.), *Woman is a Worthy Wight*, p. 70.

124. Brooke, *Medieval Idea of Marriage*, pp. 253–4.

125. Homans, *English Villagers of the Thirteenth Century*, p. 173; Hanawalt, *Ties That Bound*, pp. 203–4.

126. Goldberg, *Women, Work, and Life-Cycle in a Medieval Economy*, pp. 236, 240.

127. Helmholz, *Marriage Litigation in Medieval England*, p. 34. The deaf and dumb could therefore contract marriage by the use of signs.

128. H. A. Kelly, 'Clandestine Marriage and Chaucer's "Troilus"', *Viator*, 4 (1973), p. 443.

129. Helmholz, *Marriage Litigation in Medieval England*, pp. 35–6.

130. Pollock and Maitland, *History of English Law*, vol. 2 , pp. 368–9.
131. Helmholz, *Marriage Litigation in Medieval England*, pp. 49–57.
132. Ibid., pp. 28, 31, 62; Goldberg, *Women, Work, and Life-Cycle in a Medieval Economy*, pp. 241–3.
133. Goldberg, *Women, Work, and Life-Cycle in a Medieval Economy*, pp. 239–40; Brooke, *Medieval Idea of Marriage*, p. 251; Sheehan, *Marriage, Family, and Law in Medieval Europe*, p. 55; Helmholz, *Marriage Litigation in Medieval England*, pp. 28–9; Poos, *A Rural Society after the Black Death*, p. 139.
134. Cited in Poos, *A Rural Society after the Black Death*, p. 85.
135. Ibid., p. 138.
136. Helmholz, *Marriage Litigation in Medieval England*, pp. 29–30.
137. Homans, *English Villagers of the Thirteenth Century*, p. 164.
138. Poos, *A Rural Society after the Black Death*, p. 139.
139. *Paston Letters*, vol. 1, pp. 338, 471; H. S. Bennett, *The Pastons and Their England* (Cambridge, 1922), pp. 37–9; Richmond, 'The Pastons Revisited', pp. 26–8.
140. Helmholz, *Marriage Litigation in Medieval England*, p. 31.
141. Kelly, 'Clandestine Marriage and Chaucer's "Troilus"', pp. 438–42; Brooke, *Medieval Idea of Marriage*, p. 251; Sheehan, *Marriage, Family, and Law in Medieval Europe*, pp. 61–2.
142. Sheehan, *Marriage, Family, and Law in Medieval Europe*, pp. 46, 62.
143. C. Donahue, 'Female Plaintiffs in Marriage Cases in the Court of York in the Later Middle Ages: What Can We Learn from the Numbers?', in S. S. Walker (ed.), *Wife and Widow in Medieval England* (Michigan, 1993), pp. 183–213. See also Goldberg, '"For better for worse"', pp. 108–25; and Biller, 'Marriage Patterns and Women's Lives', pp. 60–107.
144. Helmholz, *Marriage Litigation in Medieval England*, p. 163.
145. Sheehan, *Marriage, Family, and Law in Medieval Europe*, p. 62; Kelly, 'Clandestine Marriage and Chaucer's "Troilus"', p. 440.
146. Pollock and Maitland, *History of English Law*, vol. 2, p. 425; Homans, *English Villagers of the Thirteenth Century*, pp. 177–8. For another example of a widow denied her dower because her marriage was not celebrated at the church door, see Ward (ed.), *Women of the English Nobility and Gentry*, p. 44.
147. Carlson, *Marriage and the English Reformation*, p. 33.

2　Family Life

1. Although much challenged, the classic account of courtly love, with particular reference to its manifestations in English culture, remains C. S. Lewis, *The Allegory of Love: A Study in Medieval Tradition* (Oxford, 1936).
2. G. Duby, *Love and Marriage in the Middle Ages* (Cambridge, 1994), p. 60.
3. V. L. Bullough, *Sexual Variance in Society and History* (London, 1976), pp. 379–83; Herlihy, *Medieval Households*, pp. 114, 118.
4. W. Seccombe, *Millennium of Family Change: Feudalism to Capitalism in North-*

Western Europe (London, 1995), p. 72.

5. Cited in M. M. Sheehan, *Marriage, Family and Law in Medieval Europe: Collected Studies* (Cardiff, 1996), pp. 272, 276.

6. P. P. A. Biller, 'Marriage Patterns and Women's Lives: A Sketch of a Pastoral Geography', in Goldberg (ed.), *Woman is a Worthy Wight*, pp. 69–70.

7. C. Brooke, *The Medieval Idea of Marriage* (Oxford, 1989), p. 50.

8. D. Herlihy, *Medieval Households* (Cambridge, MA, and London, 1985), pp. 118–20.

9. J. Gairdner (ed.), *The Paston Letters* (1983 edn, Gloucester), vol. 5, no. 713.

10. A. S. Haskell, 'The Paston Women on Marriage in Fifteenth-Century England', *Viator*, 4 (1973), pp. 470–1.

11. Cited in J. Bedell, 'Memory and Proof of Age in England, 1272–1327', *Past and Present*, 162 (1999), p. 13.

12. J. Ward, *English Noblewomen in the Later Middle Ages* (London, 1992), p. 29.

13. *Peter Idley's Instructions to his Son*, ed. C. D'Evelyn, Modern Language Association of America, Monograph Series, vol. VI (1935), pt I, ll. 1226–32.

14. PRO PROB 11/3/14; such phrases are found in wills of 1485 and 1496, for example, PRO PROB 11/11/2, 11/7/15.

15. From the will of Sir Thomas Cobham, 1471, where it occurs four times: PRO PROB 11/6/2.

16. S. M. Wright, *The Derbyshire Gentry in the Fifteenth Century*, Derbyshire Record Society, 8 (1983), p. 52.

17. J. Goody, *The Development of the Family and Marriage in Europe* (Cambridge, 1983), p. 206.

18. B. Hanawalt, *The Ties That Bound: Peasant Families in Medieval England* (Oxford, 1986), p. 214.

19. Brooke, *Medieval Idea of Marriage*, pp. 29–30.

20. Cited in Hanawalt, *Ties That Bound*, p. 206.

21. J. McNamara, 'Chaste Marriage and Clerical Celibacy', in V. L. Bullough and J. Brundage (eds), *Sexual Practices and the Medieval Church* (London, 1982), pp. 22–33.

22. Hanawalt, *Ties that Bound*, pp. 212–3. For Margery Kempe, see K. Ashley, 'Historicizing Margery: *The Book of Margery Kempe* as Social Text', *Journal of Medieval and Early-Modern Studies*, 28 (1998), pp. 317–88.

23. L. Betzig, 'Medieval monogamy', *Journal of Family History*, 20 (1995), pp. 181–216; Wright, *Derbyshire Gentry*, pp. 52–3. For philandering kings, see C. Given-Wilson and A. Curteis, *The Royal Bastards of Medieval England* (London, 1984).

24. N. Orme, 'The Education of the Courtier', in V. J. Scattergood and J. W. Sherborne (eds), *English Court Culture in the Later Middle Ages* (London, 1983), p. 69.

25. W. S. Holdsworth, *A History of English Law*, vol. 3 (London, 1909), pp. 395–7; F. Pollock and F. W. Maitland, *The History of English Law Before the Time of Edward I*, vol. 2, 2nd edn (Cambridge, 1968), pp. 438–9; Bedell,

'Memory and Proof of Age in England, 1272–1327', p. 6.

26. For example, in the fifteenth and early sixteenth-centuries fathers of the gentle-born William Hovington (PRO PROB 11/18/11), John Kyriel (Centre for Kentish Studies, Maidstone, PRC 32/8/51), Stephen and Walter Roberts (PRO PROB 11/4/22), Thomas Dering (Centre for Kentish Studies, PRC 32/4/154) and William Fyneaux (PRO PROB 11/22/1) all stipulated 24 as the age at which they were to enjoy full possession of their estates.

27. S. Shahar, *Childhood in the Middle Ages* (London, 1992), pp. 35–42; Hollingsworth, 'A Demographic Study of the British Ducal Families', pp. 4–26.

28. Cited in J. Le Goff, *The Birth of Purgatory* (Aldershot, 1990), p. 336; see also pp. 45, 158, 220–1, 253, 258, 265, 335, 337.

29. Hanawalt, *Ties That Bound*, p. 172; Shahar, *Childhood in the Middle Ages*, pp. 45–52.

30. Shahar, *Childhood in the Middle Ages*, pp. 14–20; Hanawalt, *Ties That Bound*, pp. 172–4.

31. Hanawalt, *Ties That Bound*, pp. 174–5. Goody, *Development of the Family and Marriage in Europe*, pp. 197–202.

32. Hanawalt, *Ties That Bound*, pp. 246–8. But for a more positive assessment of the role of godparents, see Goody, *The Development of the Family and Marriage in Europe*, p. 202; and Shahar, *Childhood in the Middle Ages*, pp. 117–18.

33. For churching, see Shahar, *Childhood in the Middle Ages*, p. 51, and Poos, *Rural Society after the Black Death*, pp. 120–7.

34. Cited in Bedell, 'Memory and Proof of Age', p. 26.

35. Ibid., pp. 13–14, 16–17.

36. Unless otherwise stated, the following account of the stages of childhood is based on Shahar, *Childhood in the Middle Ages*, pp. 21–31, 77–120; and Hanawalt, *Ties That Bound*, pp. 175–82.

37. Hanawalt, *Ties That Bound*, pp. 157–61, 175–86, 249; Shahar, *Childhood in the Middle Ages*, pp. 53–76; V. Fildes, *Wet Nursing from Antiquity to the Present* (Oxford, 1988), pp. 32–48.

38. *Paston Letters*, vol. 3, p. 123.

39. Hanawalt, *Ties That Bound*, pp. 182–3; Shahar, *Childhood in the Middle Ages*, pp. 109–11.

40. Herlihy, *Medieval Households*, p.112.

41. Biller, 'Marriage Patterns and Women's Lives', p. 82.

42. Cited in Bedell, 'Memory and Proof of Age', p. 13.

43. *Centuries of Childhood* (London, 1973), pp. 125, 356. A view challenged by, among others, Shahar, *Childhood in the Middle Ages*, pp. 95–7, 112–7, 118–20; Herlihy, *Medieval Households*, pp. 120–1, 125–7; L. C. Attreed, 'From Pearl Maiden to Tower Princes: Towards a New History of Medieval Childhood', *Journal of Medieval History*, 9 (1983), pp. 43–58.

44. D'Evelyn (ed.), *Peter Idley's Instructions to His Son*, pt II, ll. 129–40.

45. PRO PROB 11/6/15.

46. J. T. Rosenthal, *Patriarchy and Families of Privilege in Fifteenth-Century England*, (Philadelphia, PA, 1991), pp. 71–7.

47. J. C. Russell, *British Medieval Population* (Albuquerque, NM, 1948); and 'Late Medieval Population Patterns', *Speculum*, 20 (1945), pp. 157–171; J. Kraus, 'The Medieval Household: Large or Small?', *Economic History Review*, 2nd ser., 9 (1956–7), pp. 420–32; Hanawalt, *Ties That Bound*, pp. 90–5, n. 16; Z. Razi, *Life, Marriage and Death in a Medieval Parish: Economy, Society and Demography in Halesowen, 1270–1400* (Cambridge, 1980), pp. 32, 75, 85–8, 93, 139–44; C. Howell, *Land, Family and Inheritance in Transition: Kibworth Harcourt, 1280–1700* (Cambridge, 1983), pp. 232, 235. For an early modern comparison, see P. Laslett, *The World We Have Lost*, 2nd edn (Cambridge, 1971), pp. 66–7, 93, 181.

48. Seccombe, *Millennium of Family Change*, pp. 121–3.

49. Z. Razi, 'The Myth of the Immutable English Family', *Past and Present*, 140 (1993), p. 23.

50. Hanawalt, *Ties That Bound*, pp. 92–4.

51. Hollingsworth, 'A Demographic Study of British Ducal Families', pp. 4–26.

52. Howell, *Land, Family and Inheritance*, pp. 222–9. Razi, *Life, Marriage and Death in a Medieval Parish*, p. 151, found that the percentage of Halesowen tenants over 40 decreased from 65 in 1350 to only 38 in 1393.

53. A. E. Nash, 'The Mortality Pattern of the Wiltshire Lords of the Manor, 1242–1377', *Southern History*, 2 (1980), pp. 32–43.

54. Howell, *Land, Family and Inheritance*, p. 229. On average healthy couples engaged in regular sexual intercourse can produce children at about 18-month intervals: R. M. Smith, 'Marriage Processes in the English Past: Some Continuities', in L. Bonfield, R. M. Smith and K. Wrightson (eds), *The World We Have Gained: Histories of Population and Social Structure* (Oxford, 1986), p. 92.

55. Hanawalt, *Ties That Bound*, pp. 101–3. Shahar, *Childhood in the Middle Ages*, pp. 126–39.

56. P. J. Payer, *Sex and the Penitentials: The Development of a Sexual Code, 550–1150* (Toronto, 1984), pp. 23–8. The standard works on the history of contraception are, A. McLaren, *A History of Contraception from Antiquity to the Present Day* (Oxford, 1990); and J. T. Noonan, *Contraception: A History of its Treatment by the Catholic Theologians and Canonists* (Cambridge, MA, 1966).

57. See in this volume, 'Parents and Children' pp. 59–65.

58. Gottfried, *Epidemic Disease in Fifteenth-Century England*, p. 7; J. Hatcher, *Plague, Population and the English Economy* (London, 1977), pp. 55–62. The precise balance of causal factors behind demographic trends in later medieval England is highly controversial; for a recent discussion, see M. Bailey, 'Demographic Decline in Late Medieval England: Some Thoughts on Recent Research', *Economic History Review*, 2nd ser., 49 (1996), pp. 1–19.

59. Seccombe, *Millennium of Family Change*, pp. 91–4.

60. Howell, *Land, Family and Inheritance*, pp. 226–8, 235.

61. Ibid., pp. 242–3.

62. Razi, 'The Myth of the Immutable English Family', pp. 8, 23.

63. Razi, *Life, Marriage and Death in a Medieval Parish*, pp. 55, 135–6.

64. Seccombe, *Millennium of Family Change*, p. 145.
65. P. J. P. Goldberg, 'Marriage, Migration and Servanthood: The York Cause Paper Evidence', in idem (ed.), *Woman is a Worthy Wight*, pp. 1–15.
66. Goldberg, *Women, Work, and Life-Cycle*, pp. 158–202. For the sexual abuse of servants, see A. J. Kettle, 'Ruined Maids: Prostitutes and Servant Girls in Later Medieval England', in R. R. Edwards and V. Ziegler (eds), *Matrons and Marginal Women in Medieval Society* (Woodbridge, 1995), pp. 19–31.
67. Howell, *Land, Family and Inheritance*, p. 236.
68. Poos, *Rural Society after the Black Death*, pp. 212–28; Goldberg, *Women, Work, and Life-Cycle*, pp. 324–61. For Halesowen as an apparent exception, see Razi, *Life, Marriage and Death in a Medieval Parish*, p. 31. The Goldberg-Poos model has been challenged by Bailey, 'Demographic Decline in Late Medieval England', pp. 1–19.
69. Phythian-Adams, *Desolation of a City*, pp. 82–5; B. Hanawalt, '"The Childe of Bristowe" and the Making of Middle-Class Adolescence', in idem (ed.), *'Of Good and Ill Repute': Gender and Social Control in Medieval England* (Oxford, 1998), pp. 178–201.
70. Ariès, *Centuries of Childhood*, p. 354.
71. F. R. H. DuBoulay, *An Age of Ambition: English Society in the Late Middle Ages* (London, 1970), pp. 97, 100, 115, 117. The following discussion of servants in noble and gentry households is based on: P. W. Fleming, 'Household Servants of the Yorkist and Early Tudor Gentry', in D. Williams (ed.), *Early Tudor England: Proceedings of the 1987 Harlaxton Symposium* (Woodbridge, 1989), pp. 19–36; K. Mertes, *The English Noble Household, 1250–1600: Good Governance and Politic Rule* (Oxford, 1988), pp. 52–74; and C. M. Woolgar, *The Great Household in Late Medieval England* (New Haven, CT, and London, 1999), pp. 30–45.
72. J. C. Holt, 'Feudal Society and the Family in Early Medieval England: The Revolution of 1066', *Transactions of the Royal Historical Society*, 5th ser., 32 (1982), pp. 193–212.
73. G. C. Homans, *English Villagers of the Thirteenth Century*, 2nd edn (New York, 1960), pp. 187, 216–7; Hanawalt, *Ties That Bound*, pp. 79–3.
74. Holt, 'Feudal Society and the Family in Early Medieval England: The Revolution of 1066', p. 8.
75. Ibid., pp. 193–212.
76. Hanawalt, *Ties That Bound*, pp. 84–9; Laslett, *The World We Have Lost*, pp. 94–5, 181; Stone, *The Family, Sex and Marriage*, pp. 23–5.
77. Razi, 'The Myth of the Immutable English Family', pp. 19–22, 33–44. See also Seccombe, *Millennium of Family Change*, p. 82.
78. R. M. Smith, 'Kin and Neighbours in a Thirteenth-Century Suffolk Community', *Journal of Family History*, 4 (1979), p. 248; Z. Razi, 'Family, Land and the Village Community in Later Medieval England', *Past and Present*, 93 (1981), p. 17; R. J. Faith, 'Peasant Families and Inheritance Customs in Medieval England' *Agricultural History Review*, 14 (1966), pp. 86–92.
79. Razi, *Life, Marriage and Death in a Medieval Parish*, p. 69, n. 132; Bedell, 'Memory and Proof of Age in England, 1272–1327', p. 13; Hanawalt, *Ties That Bound*, p. 250; Seccombe, *Millennium of Family Change*, p. 34.

80. J. M. Bennett, 'The Tie that Binds: Peasant Marriages and Families in Late Medieval England', *Journal of Interdisciplinary History*, 15 (1984), pp. 111–29.
81. PRO PROB 11/11/2; W. E. Ball, 'The Stained-Glass Windows of Nettlestead Church', *Archaeologia Cantiana*, 28 (1894), pp. 157–249.
82. DuBoulay, *An Age of Ambition*, p. 91.
83. C. Carpenter, *Locality and Polity: A Study of Warwickshire Landed Society, 1401–1499* (Cambridge, 1992), pp. 244–62.

3 The Dissolution of Marriage and its Consequences

1. Matthew 19:6–10.
2. R. H. Helmholz, *Marriage Litigation in Medieval England* (Cambridge, 1974), pp. 74, 101.
3. Ibid., pp. 65, 81–4, 111.
4. Ibid., pp. 85–7.
5. J. T. Rosenthal, *Nobles and the Noble Life, 1295–1500* (London, 1976), p. 177; J. Ward, *English Noblewomen in the Later Middle Ages* (London, 1992), pp. 30–2.
6. Helmholz, *Marriage Litigation in Medieval England*, pp. 100–106.
7. Ibid., pp. 106–7, 220.
8. G. C. Homans, *English Villagers of the Thirteenth Century*, 2nd edn (New York, 1960), p. 174.
9. M. M. Sheehan, *Marriage, Family and Law in Medieval Europe: Collected Studies*, ed. J. K. Farge (Cardiff, 1996), p. 22.
10. J. M. Bennett, *Women in the Medieval English Countryside: Gender and Household in Brigstock Before the Plague* (Oxford, 1987), p. 144; P. Franklin, 'Peasant Widows' "Liberation" and Remarriage Before the Black Death', *Economic History Review*, 2nd ser., 39 (1986), pp. 186–204; R. H. Hilton, *The English Peasantry in the Later Middle Ages* (Oxford, 1975), pp. 99–100; B. Hanawalt, 'Remarriage as an Option for Urban and Rural Widows in Late Medieval England', in S. S. Walker (ed.), *Wife and Widow in Medieval England* (Michigan, 1993), p. 146; R. S. Gottfried, *Epidemic Disease in Fifteenth-Century England: The Medical Response and its Demographic Consequences* (New Brunswick, 1978), p. 157. J. T. Rosenthal, *Patriarchy and Families of Privilege in Fifteenth-Century England* (Philadelphia, PA, 1991), p. 182; and 'Fifteenth-Century Widows and Widowhood: Bereavement, Reintegration, and Life Choices', in S. S. Walker (ed.), *Wife and Widow in Medieval England*, pp. 42, 43. Goldberg, *Women, Work, and Life-Cycle in a Medieval Economy: Women in York and Yorkshire, c. 1300–1520* (Oxford, 1992), pp. 99, 310–11. C. Phythian-Adams, *Desolation of a City: Coventry and the Urban Crisis of the Late Middle Ages* (Cambridge, 1979), p. 92.
11. Ward, *English Noblewomen in the Later Middle Ages*, pp. 34–6; J. Kermode, *Medieval Merchants: York, Beverley and Hull in the later Middle Ages* (Cambridge, 1998), pp. 96–7, 105–10.

12. PRO C1 60/238. For examples of other Bristol widows refusing to act or denying responsibility, see C1 45/307; 530/12. P. Fleming and K. Costello, *Discovering Cabot's Bristol: Life in the Medieval and Tudor Town* (Tiverton, 1998), p. 39.

13. PRO C1 61/542.

14. F. Pollock and F. W. Maitland, *The History of English Law Before the Time of Edward I*, vol. 2, 2nd edn (Cambridge, 1968), pp. 348–56.

15. For example, in fifteenth-century Kent, the gentlemen John Digges and John Alfegh allowed their wives to have the goods they had brought to their marriages: Centre for Kentish Studies, Maidstone, PRC 32/7/66; PRO PROB 11/8/18. Rosenthal, *Patriarchy and Families of Privilege*, pp. 187–90.

16. E. W. W. Veale, *The Great Red Book of Bristol*, vol. 1, *Introduction: Burgage Tenure in Mediaeval Bristol*, Bristol Record Society, vol. 2 (1931), pp.71–2; Kermode, *Medieval Merchants*, pp. 93–4; K. E. Lacey, 'Women and Work in Fourteenth- and Fifteenth-century London', in L. Charles and L. Duffin (eds), *Women and Work in Pre-Industrial England* (London, 1985), pp. 36–8.

17. Lacey, 'Women and Work in Fourteenth- and Fifteenth-century London', pp. 37–8.

18. Veale, *Great Red Book of Bristol*, vol. 1, pp. 22–5, 47–55, 109–11, 263.

19. W. S. Holdsworth, *A History of English Law*, vol. 3 (London, 1909), p. 260.

20. Bennett, *Women in the Medieval English Countryside*, p. 144. Hanawalt, 'Remarriage as an option for urban and rural widows in late medieval England', p. 147; and *Ties That Bound*, pp. 221–2.

21. J. A. Raftis, *Tenure and Mobility: Studies in the Social history of the Medieval English Village* (Toronto, 1964), pp. 36, 39; E. B. Fryde, *Peasants and Landlords in Later Medieval England* (Stroud, 1996), pp. 213–14, 218–19, 269.

22. R. Archer, '"Rich Old Ladies": The Problem of Late Medieval Dowagers', in A. J. Pollard (ed.), *Property and Politics: Essays in Later Medieval English History* (Gloucester, 1984), p. 18.

23. Ward, *English Noblewomen in the Later Middle Ages*, p. 36; Rosenthal, *Patriarchy and Families of Privilege*, pp. 198–9.

24. PRO PROB 11/10/32.

25. For example, see the will of Sir Edward Poynings, 1521 (PRO PROB 11/20/21). S. M. Wright, *The Derbyshire Gentry in the Fifteenth Century*, Derbyshire Record Society, 8 (1983), pp. 70, 85.

26. Hanawalt, 'Remarriage as an Option for Urban and Rural Widows in Late Medieval England', p. 145.

27. J. Ward (ed.), *Women of the English Nobility and Gentry, 1066–1500* (Manchester, 1995), p. 44.

28. S. S. Walker, 'Litigation as Personal Quest: Suing for Dower in the Royal Courts, c. 1272–1350', in idem (ed.), *Wife and Widow in Medieval England*, pp. 81–108.

29. Ward (ed.), *Women of the English Nobility and Gentry*, pp. 61–3; Pollock and Maitland, *History of English Law*, vol. 2, pp. 395–6.

30. Archer, '"Rich Old Ladies"', p. 20. Rosenthal, *Nobles and the Noble Life*,

pp. 140–1; and *Patriarchy and Families of Privilege*, pp. 194–5. C. Given-Wilson, *The English Nobility in the Later Middle Ages: The Fourteenth-Century Political Community* (London, 1987), p. 139, n. 51. The law signally failed to protect dowagers during the thirteenth-century Barons' Wars and the period of Despenser dominance: P. Dobrowolski, 'Women and their Dower in the Long Thirteenth Century, 1265–1329', in M. Prestwich, R. H. Britnell and R. Frame (eds), *Thirteenth-Century England: Proceedings of the Durham Conference* (Woodbridge, 1997), pp. 157–64. See also Ward, *English Noblewomen in the Later Middle Ages*, pp. 44–8, which provides a detailed discussion of the fate of widows of the rebels in the 1320s.

31. J. R. Lander, 'Attainder and Forfeiture, 1453–1509', in idem, *Crown and Nobility, 1450–1509* (London, 1976), pp. 127–58.

32. Archer, '"Rich Old Ladies"', p. 20.

33. C. Ross, *Richard III* (London, 1981), p. 117; *Calendar of Patent Rolls*, 1476–85, pp. 406, 515, 525. *Calendar of Close Rolls*, 1476–85, no. 1301. R. Horrox and P. W. Hammond (eds), *British Library Harleian Manuscript 433*, vol. i, pp. 135, 152, 207; vol. ii, p. 77. PRO C67/51.

34. Archer, '"Rich Old Ladies"', pp. 16–7.

35. J. S. Leongard, '*Rationabilis dos*: Magna Carta and the Widow's "Fair Share" in the Earlier Thirteenth Century', in Walker (ed.), *Wife and Widow in Medieval England*, pp. 59–80.

36. Archer, '"Rich Old Ladies"', p. 22. And for further examples, see Ward, *English Noblewomen in the Later Middle Ages*, pp. 43–4.

37. Unless otherwise indicated, this and the following two paragraphs are based on K. B. McFarlane, *The Nobility of Later Medieval England* (Oxford, 1973), pp. 65, 153; and Archer, '"Rich Old Ladies"', pp. 15–35.

38. Rosenthal, *Patriarchy and Families of Privilege*, p. 197; Ward, *English Noblewomen in the Later Middle Ages*, p. 37.

39. *Troilus and Criseyde*, ll. 750–4, cited in C. Brooke, *The Medieval Idea of Marriage* (Oxford, 1989), p. 222.

40. Ff. Swabey, *Medieval Gentlewoman: Life in a Widow's Household in the Later Middle Ages* (Stroud, 1999).

41. M. W. Labarge, 'Three Medieval Widows and a Second Career', in M. M. Sheehan (ed.), *Aging and the Aged in Medieval Europe* (Toronto, 1990), pp. 159–72; J. T. Rosenthal, 'Fifteenth-Century Widows and Widowhood: Bereavement, Reintegration, and Life Choices', in Walker (ed), *Wife and Widow in Medieval England*, pp. 44–5.

42. Hanawalt, 'Remarriage as an Option for Urban and Rural Widows in Late Medieval England', pp. 158–9; Fleming and Costello, *Discovering Cabot's Bristol*, pp. 36–9; Goldberg, *Women, Work, and Life-Cycle in a Medieval Economy*, pp. 309–18; Phythian-Adams, *Desolation of a City*, p. 92. For studies of London widows, see C. M. Barron and A. F. Sutton (eds), *Medieval London Widows, 1300–1500* (London, 1994).

43. Franklin, 'Peasant Widows' "Liberation" and Remarriage Before the Black Death', p. 202; Smith, 'Some Reflections on the Evidence for the Origins of the "European Marriage Pattern" in England', p. 96; Bennett, *Women in the Medieval English Countryside*, pp. 76, 142–6, 149, 152, 160, 172, 176; Hanawalt, *Ties That Bound*, pp. 223–5.

Notes to Pages 95–9

44. Lucy Pofot met a stranger at a tavern and had sex with him, and was found the next morning with five knife wounds. Sarra, a 46-year-old widow, entertained three men at her house who then killed and robbed her: Hanawalt, *Ties That Bound*, p. 226.
45. Ibid., p. 222; J. A. Brundage, 'Widows and Remarriage: Moral Conflicts and their Resolution in Classical Common Law', in Walker (ed.), *Wife and Widow in Medieval England*, pp. 17–31; Hanawalt, 'Remarriage as an Option for Urban and Rural Widows in Late Medieval England', pp. 142–3.
46. Hanawalt, 'Remarriage as an Option for Urban and Rural Widows in Late Medieval England', p. 160; and *Ties That Bound*, p. 225; Kermode, *Medieval Merchants*, p. 94; Rosenthal, *Patriarchy and Families of Privilege*, pp. 190–2.
47. Goldberg, *Women, Work, and Life-Cycle in a Medieval Economy*, p. 273.
48. Smith, 'Some Reflections on the Evidence for the Origins of the "European Marriage Pattern" in England', pp. 93–5; Bennett, *Women in the Medieval English Countryside*, p. 147. Hanawalt, 'Remarriage as an Option for Urban and Rural Widows in Late Medieval England', p. 148; and *Ties That Bound*, p. 224. Z. Razi, *Life, Marriage and Death in a Medieval Parish: Economy, Society and Demography in Halesowen, 1270–1400* (Cambridge, 1980), p. 138.
49. Phythian-Adams, *Desolation of a City*, pp. 199–201. Goldberg, *Women, Work, and Life-Cycle in a Medieval Economy*, pp. 280–304, 324–61. In York between 1389 and 1520, around 15 per cent of the more prosperous widows remarried, less than half the figure for prosperous widowers: ibid., p. 267.
50. Franklin, 'Peasant Widows' "Liberation" and Remarriage Before the Black Death', pp. 202–4; Rosenthal, 'Fifteenth-Century Widows and Widowhood: Bereavement, Reintegration, and Life Choices', pp. 51–2. Hanawalt, *Ties That Bound*, p. 225; and 'Remarriage as an Option for Urban and Rural Widows in Late Medieval England', p. 159.
51. Hanawalt, 'Remarriage as an Option for Urban and Rural Widows in Late Medieval England', pp. 154–7; Kermode, *Medieval Merchants*, p. 91.
52. Rosenthal, *Patriarchy and Families of Privilege*, pp. 213–4.
53. Archer, '"Rich Old Ladies"', pp. 27–8; Ward (ed.), *Women of the English Nobility and Gentry*, p. 43.
54. R. A. Griffiths and R. S. Thomas, *The Making of the Tudor Dynasty* (Gloucester, 1985), pp. 30–1 .
55. M. K. Jones and M. G. Underwood, *The King's Mother: Lady Margaret Beaufort, Countess of Richmond and Derby* (Cambridge, 1992), pp. 38–9,
56. Ibid., *passim*, but particularly pp. 252–6; Griffiths and Thomas, *The Making of the Tudor Dynasty*, pp. 36–7.
57. J. R. Lander, 'Marriage and Politics in the Fifteenth Century: The Nevilles and the Wydevilles', in idem, *Crown and Nobility*, pp. 94–126.
58. The decision to remarry or remain single was usually taken within a year of their husbands' deaths. Rosenthal, 'Fifteenth-Century Widows and Widowhood: Bereavement, Reintegration, and Life Choices', pp. 36–7, 42.

59. Archer, '"Rich Old Ladies"', pp. 24–5; McFarlane, *Nobility of Later Medieval England*, p. 153; Rosenthal, *Patriarchy and Families of Privilege*, pp. 208–9; J. R. Lander, *The Wars of the Roses* (London, 1965), p. 145.

60. Rosenthal, *Patriarchy and Families of Privilege*, pp. 208–11.

61. E. J. Carlson, *Marriage and the English Reformation* (Oxford, 1994), pp. 25–6; J. C. Holt, 'Feudal Society and the Family in Early Medieval England: The Heiress and the Alien', *Transactions of the Royal Historical Society*, 5th ser., 35 (1985), p. 21; Archer, '"Rich Old Ladies"', pp. 16–17.

62. Archer, '"Rich Old Ladies"', p. 27. Rosenthal, *Patriarchy and Families of Privilege*, pp. 212–13; and *Nobles and the Noble Life*, pp. 139, 174–5. Ward (ed.), *Women of the English Nobility and Gentry*, p. 42.

63. Ward (ed.), *Women of the English Nobility and Gentry*, pp. 41–2, for this and the following paragraph.

64. Rosenthal, *Patriarchy and Families of Privilege*, pp. 175–246 provides a sensitive discussion of widowhood as it may have affected widows.

65. Painter, 'The Family and the Feudal System in Twelfth-Century England', p. 13; Pollock and Maitland, *History of English Law*, vol. 2, pp. 414–8, 428–9; Homans, *English Villagers of the Thirteenth Century*, pp. 184–9.

66. J. T. Rosenthal, 'Heirs' Ages and Family Succession in Yorkshire, 1399–1422', *Yorkshire Archaeological Journal*, 56 (1984), pp. 87–94; and *Patriarchy and Families of Privilege*, p. 38.

67. The standard work on royal wardship is S. L. Waugh, *The Lordship of England: Royal Wardships and Marriage in English Society and Politics, 1217–1327* (Princeton, NJ, 1988), on which this section is based unless otherwise indicated. S. F. C. Milson, 'The Origin of Prerogative Wardship', in G. Garnett and J. Hudson (eds), *Law and Government in Medieval England and Normandy* (Cambridge, 1994), pp. 223–4; S. S. Walker, 'Widow and Ward: The Feudal Law of Child Custody in Medieval England', in S. M. Stuard (ed.), *Women in Medieval Society* (Pennsylvania, 1976), pp. 159–72.

68. McFarlane, *Nobility of Later Medieval England*, pp. 76–8, 217–19; Given-Wilson, *English Nobility in the Late Middle Ages*, pp. 149–51; S. Payling, 'The Politics of Family: Late Medieval Marriage Contracts', in R. H. Britnell and A. J. Pollard (eds), *The McFarlane Legacy: Studies in Late Medieval Politics and Society* (Stroud and New York, 1995), p. 24; I. Pinchbeck and M. Hewitt, *Children in English Society* (London, 1969), vol. 1, p. 12; Wright, *Derbyshire Gentry*, pp. 38–42.

69. Wright, *Derbyshire Gentry*, pp. 38–40.

70. J. M. W. Bean, *The Decline of English Feudalism, 1215–1540* (Manchester, 1968), pp. 197, 220–34.

71. Ward, *Women of the English Nobility and Gentry*, p. 37; Walker, 'Widow and ward', pp. 160–1; Rosenthal, *Nobles and the Noble Life*, p. 140.

72. Rosenthal, *Nobles and the Noble Life*, pp. 136–7; Holt, 'Feudal Society and the Family in Early Medieval England: The Heiress and the Alien', p. 21.

73. J. Gairdner (ed.), *The Paston Letters* (1983 edn, Gloucester), vol. 1, p. 615.

74. *Calendar of Fine Rolls, 1471–1485*, no. 782; *Calendar of Inquisitions Post*

Mortem for the Reign of Henry VII, vol. 1, p. 616.

75. *Calendar of Patent Rolls, 1485–1494*, p. 167; *Calendar of Inquisitions Post Mortem for the Reign of Henry VII*, vol. 2, p. 193, vol. 3, p. 207; R. C. Jenkins, 'The Family of Guildford', *Archaeologia Cantiana*, 14 (1882), pp. 1–17.

76. C. Richmond, *The Paston Family in the Fifteenth Century: The First Phase* (Cambridge, 1990), p. 124.

77. PRO Early Chancery Proceedings, C1/102/63.

78. *Paston Letters*, vol. 1, pp. 154–5. For John Wyndham, another member of the Paston circle who thought little of selling one of his children, see Richmond, *The Paston Family in the Fifteenth Century: The First Phase*, p. 220.

79. Walker, 'Widow and Ward: The Feudal Law of Child Custody in Medieval England', p. 166.

80. Carlson, *Marriage and the English Reformation*, p. 28; Rosenthal, *Nobles and the Noble Life*, p. 176.

81. Ward, *Women of the English Nobility and Gentry*, pp. 21–2.

82. Carlson, *Marriage and the English Reformation*, p. 28, n. 151.

83. Cited in Hanawalt, *Ties That Bound*, p. 248.

84. Ibid., pp. 248–9.

85. Homans, *English Villagers of the Thirteenth Century*, pp. 191–3.

86. Pollock and Maitland, *History of English Law*, vol. 2, pp. 283–4.

87. PRO, C1/102/63.

88. Wright, *Derbyshire Gentry*, p. 39.

89. PRO, C1/26/304; F. W. T. Attree and J. H. L. Booker, 'The Sussex Colepepers', *Sussex Archaeological Collections*, 47 (1904), pp. 47–81; 48 (1905), pp. 65–98; PRO PROB 11/18/24.

90. PRO, C1/298/3.

91. Hanawalt, *Ties That Bound*, pp. 250–1.

92. PRO PROB 11/22/6; 11/22/21. For a broad perspective on this issue, see J. Boswell, *The Kindness of Strangers: The Abandonment of Children in Western Europe from Late Antiquity to the Renaissance* (New York, 1988).

93. D. Herlihy, 'The Family and Religious Ideologies in Medieval Europe' in T. Hareven and A. Plakans (eds), *Family History at the Crossroads* (Princeton, NJ, 1987), pp. 9–10; J. Goody, *The Development of the Family and Marriage in Europe* (Cambridge, 1983), p. 121. Holt, 'Feudal Society and the Family in Early Medieval England: The Heiress and the Alien', pp. 1–28; and 'Feudal Society and the Family in Early Medieval England: Notions of Patrimony', *Transactions of the Royal Historical Society*, 5th ser., 33 (1983), p. 206.

94. Goody, *Development of the Family and Marriage in Europe*, pp. 119–20; Holt, 'Feudal Society and the Family in Early Medieval England: The Revolution of 1066', pp. 193–212; Painter, 'The Family and the Feudal System in Twelfth-Century England', pp. 8–11.

95. C. Howell, *Land, Family and Inheritance in Transition: Kibworth Harcourt, 1280–1700* (Cambridge, 1983), pp. 239n, 240n; F. Hull, 'The Customal of Kent', *Archaeologia Cantiana*, 72 (1958), pp. 148–59. G. C. Homans, 'Partible Inheritance of Villagers' Holdings', *Economic History Review*, vol. 8 (1937–8), pp. 48–56; and *English Villagers of the Thirteenth Century*, pp.

109–18, 123–7. T. M. Charles-Edwards, 'Kinship, Status and the Origins of the Hide', *Past and Present*, 56 (1972), pp. 29, 32; W. Seccombe, *Millennium of Family Change: Feudalism to Capitalism in North-Western Europe* (London, 1995), pp. 39, 63–4; Hanawalt, *Ties that Bound*, pp. 69–70; C. Howell, 'Peasant Inheritance Customs in the Midlands, 1280–1700', in J. Goody, J. Thirk and E. P. Thomson (eds), *Family and Inheritance: Rural Society in Western Europe, 1200–1800* (Cambridge, 1976), p. 116; R. Faith, 'Peasant Families and Inheritance Customs in Medieval England', *Agricultural History Review*, 14 (1966), pp. 86–92; Raftis, *Tenure and Mobility*, p. 56.

96. Raftis, *Tenure and Mobility*, pp. 46–7; Homans, *English Villagers of the Thirteenth Century*, pp. 133–5, 141–2.

97. Homans, *English Villagers of the Thirteenth Century*, pp. 195–9; Painter, 'The Family and the Feudal System in Twelfth-Century England', p. 4; Raftis, *Tenure and Mobility*, pp. 60–2.

98. Howell, *Land, Family and Inheritance in Transition*, pp. 238–9; Hanawalt, *Ties That Bound*, pp. 75–6; Seccombe, *Millennium of Family Change*, p. 101; Razi, *Life, Marriage and Death in a Medieval Parish*, pp. 50–1; Homans, *English Villagers of the Thirteenth Century*, pp. 129–32, 137–8; Hilton, *English Peasants in the Later Middle Ages*, pp. 100–1.

99. Smith, 'Some Reflections on the Evidence for the Origins of the "European Marriage Pattern" in England', p. 93; 'Some Issues Concerning Families and their Property in Rural England, 1250–1800', in idem (ed.), *Land, Kinship and Life-Cycle* (Cambridge, 1984), pp. 53–4; idem, 'Families and their Land in an Area of Partible Inheritance: Redgrave, Suffolk, 1260–1320', in ibid., pp. 135–95. Seccombe, *Millennium of Family Change*, pp. 96–100; B. Hanawalt, *Ties That Bound*, pp. 68–75.

100. Razi, *Life, Marriage and Death in a Medieval Parish*, pp. 135–6; Seccombe, *Millennium of Family Change*, pp. 146–7; J. Ravensdale, 'Population Change and the Transfer of Customary Land on a Cambridgeshire Manor in the Fourteenth Century', in Smith (ed.), *Land, Kinship and Life-Cycle*, pp. 223–4; C. Dyer, 'Changes in the Size of Peasant Holdings in some West Midlands Villages, 1400–1540', in ibid., p. 285.

101. Homans, *English Villagers of the Thirteenth Century*, pp. 122–3; Razi, 'Family, Land and the Village Community in Later Medieval England', *Past and Present*, 93 (1981), pp. 26–7.

102. J. C. Holt, 'Feudal Society and the Family in Early Medieval England: Patronage and Politics', *Transactions of the Royal Historical Society*, 5th ser., 34 (1984), pp. 15–16; Painter, 'The Family and the Feudal system in Twelfth-Century England', pp. 9–10; H. M. Thomas, *Vassals, Heiresses, Crusaders and Thugs: The Gentry of Angevin Yorkshire, 1154–1216* (Philadelphia, PA, 1993), pp. 115–27.

103. The phrase comes from Seccombe, *Millennium of Family Change*, p. 39.

104. For example, in the fifteenth century the Bettenham family of Kent included esquires, gentleman, and at least one yeoman, Stephen. Both this Stephen and his namesake, a gentleman and great-grandson of another Stephen (d.1415), esquire and JP, were tenants of the manor of

Glassenbury in 1482: E. F. Jacob (ed.), *The Register of Henry Chichele, Archbishop of Canterbury, 1414–43*, vol. 2, Canterbury and York Soc. (1940), p. 641; British Library, Harleian Charters 76/G/57; PRO C1/32/80, C1/41/48; Centre for Kentish Studies, Maidstone, U47/11/8. See also P. Laslett, *The World We Have Lost*, 2nd edn (Cambridge, 1971), p. 196.

105. Carpenter, *Locality and Polity*, pp. 244–62. A. J. Pollard, *North-Eastern England During the Wars of the Roses*, pp. 100–10; Rosenthal, *Patriarchy and Families of Privilege*, pp. 23–77; Thomas, *Vassals, Heiresses, Crusaders and Thugs*, pp. 127–30; Rosenthal, *Nobles and the Noble Life*, pp. 137–8; S. J. Payling, 'Social Mobility, Demographic Change, and Landed Society in Late Medieval England', *Economic History Review*, 45 (1992), pp. 51–73.

106. E. A. Wrigley, 'Fertility Strategy for the Individual and the Group', in C. Tilly (ed.), *Historical Studies of Changing Fertility* (Princeton, NJ, 1978), p. 139; Gottfried, *Epidemic Disease in Fifteenth-Century England*, pp. 177, 191–5, 221; Waugh, *Lordship of England*, pp. 15–22.

107. J. P. Cooper, 'Patterns of Inheritance and Settlement by Great Landowners from the Fifteenth to the Eighteenth Centuries', in J. Goody, J. Thirsk and E. P. Thompson (eds), *Family and Inheritance: Rural Society in Western Europe, 1200–1800* (Cambridge, 1976), p. 300.

108. McFarlane, *Nobility of Later Medieval England*, pp. 270–4; Given-Wilson, *English Nobility in the Late Middle Ages*, p. 143; Payling, 'Social Mobility, Demographic Change, and Landed Society in Late Medieval England', pp. 56–62; Carpenter, *Locality and Polity*, pp. 248–51; Wright, *Derbyshire Gentry*, pp. 29–32, 35–8.

109. PRO PROB 11/16/12.

110. Seccombe, *Millennium of Family Change*, pp. 102–3; Goody, *Development of the Family and Marriage in Europe*, pp. 123–5; P. W. Fleming, 'The Lovelace Dispute: Concepts of Property and Inheritance in Fifteenth-Century Kent', *Southern History*, 12 (1990), pp. 1–18.

111. Painter, 'The Family and the Feudal System in Twelfth-Century England', p. 9; PRO PROB 11/21/7. In addition, in 1446 Stephen Cossington left 20 marks to his daughter if she became a nun (Centre for Kentish Studies, Maidstone, PRC 32/1/62), and in 1511 John Toke's daughter would receive £10 if she took the veil (PRO PROB 11/17/18).

112. PRO PROB 11/20/21. An eighteenth-century historian of Kent claimed that Sir Edward had four mistresses: E. Hasted, *The History and Topographical Survey of the County of Kent* 2nd edn (Wakefield, 1972), vol. 8, p. 72. S. Shahar, *The Fourth Estate: A History of Women in the Middle Ages* (London, 1983), pp. 113–20; Wright, *Derbyshire Gentry*, pp. 52–3.

113. S. Shahar, *Growing Old in the Middle Ages* (London, 1997), pp. 88–97.

114. Homans, *English Villagers of the Thirteenth Century*, pp.144–8; Howell, *Land, Family and Inheritance in Transition*, pp. 244–8; E. Clark, 'The Quest for Security in Medieval England', in M. M. Sheehan (ed.), *Ageing and the Aged in Medieval Europe* (Toronto, 1990), pp. 189–200.

115. E. Clark, 'Some Aspects of Social Security in Medieval England', *Journal of Family History*, 7 (1982), pp. 307–20.

116. Hanawalt, *Ties That Bound*, pp. 229–30.

117. Dyer 'Changes in the Size of Peasant Holdings in some West Midlands Villages', p. 289.
118. Homans, *English Villagers of the Thirteenth Century*, pp. 150–6; A. Macfarlane, *The Origins of English Individualism: The Family, Property and Social Transition* (Oxford, 1978), pp. 141–4.
119. Hanawalt, *Ties That Bound*, p. 229–36.

Conclusion

1. J. Bedell, 'Memory and Proof of Age in England, 1272–1327', *Past and Present*, 162 (1999), pp. 21–2.
2. G. C. Homans, *English Villagers of the Thirteenth Century*, 2nd edn (New York, 1960), p. 218.
3. P. Laslett, *The World We Have Lost*, 2nd edn (Cambridge, 1971), p. 94.
4. Z. Razi, 'Family, Land and the Village Community in Later Medieval England', *Past and Present*, 93 (1981), pp. 20–2; W. Seccombe, *Millennium of Family Change: Feudalism to Capitalism in North-Western Europe* (London, 1995), p. 38.
5. R. H. Helmholz, *Marriage Litigation in Medieval England* (Cambridge, 1974), p. 25.
6. R. M. Smith, 'Marriage Processes in the English Past: Some Continuities', in L. Bonfield, R. M. Smith and K. Wrightson (eds), *The World We Have Gained: Histories of Population and Social Structure* (Oxford, 1986), pp. 90–2.
7. A. Macfarlane, *The Origins of English Individualism: The Family, Property and Social Transition* (Oxford, 1978).

SELECT BIBLIOGRAPHY

Archer, Rowena, '"Rich Old Ladies": The Problem of Late Medieval Dowagers', in A. J. Pollard (ed.), *Property and Politics: Essays in Later Medieval English History* (Gloucester, 1984), pp. 15–35.

Ariès, Philippe, *Centuries of Childhood* (London, 1973).

Bailey, Mark, 'Demographic Decline in Late Medieval England: Some Thoughts on Recent Research', *Economic History Review*, 2nd ser., 49 (1996), pp. 1–19.

Barron, Caroline M., and Sutton, Anne F. (eds), *Medieval London Widows, 1300–1500* (London, 1994).

Bean, J. M. W., *The Decline of English Feudalism, 1215–1540* (Manchester, 1968).

Bedell, J., 'Memory and Proof of Age in England, 1272–1327', *Past and Present*, 162 (1999), pp. 3–27.

Bennett, Judith M., *Women in the Medieval English Countryside: Gender and Household in Brigstock Before the Plague* (Oxford, 1987).

Biller, P. P. A., 'Marriage Patterns and Women's Lives: A Sketch of a Pastoral Geography', in P. J. P Goldberg (ed.), *Woman is a Worthy Wight: Women in English Society, c.1200–1500* (Stroud, 1992), pp. 60–107.

Brand, P. A., Hyams, P., and Faith, R., 'Debate: Seigneurial Control of Women's Marriage', *Past and Present*, 99 (1983), pp. 123–48.

Brooke, Christopher, *The Medieval Idea of Marriage* (Oxford, 1989).

Brundage, J. A., *Sex, Law and Marriage in the Middle Ages* (Aldershot, 1993).

Carlson, E. J., *Marriage and the English Reformation* (Oxford, 1994).

Carpenter, Christine, *Locality and Polity: A Study of Warwickshire Landed Society, 1401–1499* (Cambridge, 1992).

Dockray, Keith, 'Why did Fifteenth-Century English Gentry Marry? The Pastons, Plumptons and Stonors Reconsidered', in M. Jones (ed.), *Gentry and Lesser Nobility in Later Medieval Europe* (Gloucester, 1986), pp. 61–80.

DuBoulay, F. R. H., *An Age of Ambition: English Society in the Late Middle Ages* (London, 1970).

Duby, Georges, *Medieval Marriage: Two Models from Twelfth-Century France* (Baltimore, MD, 1978).

The Knight, the Lady and the Priest: The Making of Marriage in Medieval France (Harmondsworth, 1983).

Love and Marriage in the Middle Ages (Cambridge, 1994).

Dyer, Christopher, *Lords and Peasants in a Changing Society* (Cambridge, 1980).

Faith, Rosamund, 'Peasant Families and Inheritance Customs in Medieval England', *Agricultural History Review*, 14 (1966), pp. 77–95.

Franklin, P., 'Peasant Widows' "Liberation" and Remarriage Before the Black Death', *Economic History Review*, 2nd ser., 39 (1986), pp. 186–204.

Fryde, E. B., *Peasants and Landlords in Later Medieval England* (Stroud, 1996).

Gairdner, James (ed.), *The Paston Letters* (1983 edn, Gloucester).

Given-Wilson, Christopher, *The English Nobility in the Late Middle Ages: The Fourteenth-Century Political Community* (London, 1987).

Goldberg, P. J. P., *Women, Work and Life-Cycle in a Medieval Economy: Women in York and Yorkshire, c.1300–1520* (Oxford, 1992).

(ed.), *Woman is a Worthy Wight: Women in English Society, c.1200–1500* (Stroud, 1992).

'"For Better for Worse": Marriage and Economic Opportunity for Women in Town and Country', in idem (ed.), *Woman is a Worthy Wight: Women in English Society, c.1200–1500* (Stroud, 1992), pp. 108–25.

Goody, Jack, Thirsk, Joan and Thompson, Edward P. (eds), *Family and Inheritance: Rural Society in Western Europe, 1200–1800* (Cambridge, 1976).

Goody, Jack, *The Development of the Family and Marriage in Europe* (Cambridge, 1983).

Gottfried, R. S., *Epidemic Disease in Fifteenth-Century England: The Medical Response and the Demographic Consequences* (New Brunswick, 1978).

Hanawalt, Barbara, *The Ties That Bound: Peasant Families in Medieval England* (Oxford, 1986).

'Remarriage as an Option for Urban and Rural Widows in Late Medieval England', in S. S. Walker (ed.), *Wife and Widow in Medieval England* (Michigan, 1993), pp. 141–64.

Haskell, A., 'The Paston Women on Marriage in Fifteenth-Century England', *Viator*, 4 (1973), pp. 459–69.

Helmholz, Richard H., *Marriage Litigation in Medieval England* (Cambridge, 1974).

Herlihy, David, *Medieval Households* (London, 1985).

'The Family and Religious Ideologies in Medieval Europe', in T. Hareven and A. Plakans (eds), *Family History at the Crossroads* (Princeton, NJ, 1987), pp. 3–17.

Hilton, Rodney H., *The English Peasantry in the Later Middle Ages* (Oxford, 1975).

Hollingsworth, T. H., 'A Demographic Study of British Ducal Families', *Population Studies*, 11 (1958 for 1957–8), pp. 4–26.

Holt, J. C., 'Feudal Society and the Family in Early Medieval England:

The Revolution of 1066', *Transactions of the Royal Historical Society*, 5th ser., 32 (1982), pp. 193–212.

'Feudal Society and the Family in Early Medieval England: Notions of Patrimony', *Transactions of the Royal Historical Society*, 5th ser., 33 (1983), pp. 193–220.

'Feudal Society and the Family in Early Medieval England: Patronage and Politics', *Transactions of the Royal Historical Society*, 5th ser., 34 (1984), pp. 1–25.

'Feudal Society and the Family in Early Medieval England: The Heiress and the alien', *Transactions of the Royal Historical Society*, 5th ser., 35 (1985), pp. 1–28.

Homans, G. C., *English Villagers of the Thirteenth Century*, 2nd edn (New York, 1960).

Howell, C., *Land, Family and Inheritance in Transition: Kibworth Harcourt, 1280–1700* (Cambridge, 1983).

Kelly, H. A., 'Clandestine Marriage and Chaucer's "Troilus"', *Viator*, 4 (1973), pp. 435–57.

Kermode, Jennifer, *Medieval Merchants: York, Beverley and Hull in the Later Middle Ages* (Cambridge, 1998).

Lander, Jack R., *Crown and Nobility, 1450–1509* (London, 1976).

Laslett, Peter, *The World We Have Lost*, 2nd edn (Cambridge, 1971).

Macfarlane, Alan M., *The Origins of English Individualism: The Family, Property and Social Transition* (Oxford, 1978).

McFarlane, K. B., *The Nobility of Later Medieval England* (Oxford, 1973).

Mate, Mavis, *Women in English Society* (Cambridge, 1999).

Mertes, Kate, *The English Noble Household, 1250–1600: Good Governance and Politic Rule* (Oxford, 1988).

Painter, Sidney, 'The Family and the Feudal System in Twelfth-Century England', *Speculum*, 35 (1960), pp. 1–16.

Payling, Simon, 'Social Mobility, Demographic Change and Landed Society in Later Medieval England', *Economic History Review*, 45 (1992), pp. 51–73.

'The Politics of Family: Late Medieval Marriage Contracts', in R. H. Britnell and A. J. Pollard (eds), *The McFarlane Legacy: Studies in Late Medieval Politics and Society* (Stroud, 1995), pp. 21–47.

Phythian-Adams, Charles, *Desolation of a City: Coventry and the Urban Crisis of the Late Middle Ages* (Cambridge, 1979).

Pollard, Anthony J., *North-Eastern England During the Wars of the Roses: Lay Society, War and Politics, 1450–1500* (Oxford, 1990).

Pollock, F., and Maitland, F.W., *The History of English Law Before the Time of Edward I*, 2 vols, 2nd edn (Cambridge, 1968).

Poos, L. R., *A Rural Society after the Black Death: Essex, 1350–1525* (Cambridge, 1991).

Raftis, J. A., *Tenure and Mobility: Studies in the Social History of the Medieval*

English Village (Toronto, 1964).

Razi, Zvi, *Life, Marriage and Death in a Medieval Parish: Economy, Society and Demography in Halesowen, 1270–1400* (Cambridge, 1980).

'The Myth of the Immutable English Family', *Past and Present*, 140 (1993), pp. 3–44.

Richmond, Colin, 'The Pastons Revisited: Marriage and the Family in Fifteenth-Century England', *Bulletin of the Institute of Historical Research*, 58 (1985), pp. 25–36.

The Paston Family in the Fifteenth Century: The First Phase (Cambridge, 1990).

The Paston Family in the Fifteenth Century: Fastolf's Will (Cambridge, 1996).

Rosenthal, Joel T. (ed.), *Nobles and the Noble Life, 1295–1500* (London, 1976).

Patriarchy and Families of Privilege in Fifteenth-Century England (Philadelphia, PA, 1991).

'Fifteenth-Century Widows and Widowhood: Bereavement, Re-integration, and Life Choices', in S. S. Walker (ed.), *Wife and Widow in Medieval England* (Michigan, 1993), pp. 33–58.

Searle, Eleanor, 'Seigneurial Control of Women's Marriage: The Antecedents and Function of Merchet in Medieval England', *Past and Present*, 82 (1979), pp. 3–43.

Seccombe, Wally, *A Millennium of Family Change: Feudalism to Capitalism in North-Western Europe* (London, 1995).

Shahar, Shulamith, *Childhood in the Middle Ages* (London, 1992).

Growing Old in the Middle Ages (London, 1997).

Sheehan, Michael M., *Ageing and the Aged in Medieval Europe* (Toronto, 1990).

Marriage, Family and Law in Medieval Europe: Collected Studies, ed. J. K. Farge (Cardiff, 1996).

Smith, Richard M., 'Some Reflections on the Evidence for the Origins of the "European Marriage Pattern" in England', in C. Harris (ed.), *The Sociology of the Family: New Directions for Britain* (Keele, 1979), pp. 74–112.

(ed.), *Land, Kinship and Life-Cycle* (Cambridge, 1984).

'Marriage Processes in the English Past: Some Continuities', in L. Bonfield, R. M. Smith and K. Wrightson (eds), *The World We Have Gained: Histories of Population and Social Structure* (Oxford, 1986), pp. 43–98.

Stone, Lawrence, *The Family, Sex and Marriage in England, 1500–1800* (London, 1977).

Stuard, S. M. (ed.), *Women in Medieval Society* (Philadelphia, PA, 1976).

Swabey, ffiona, *Medieval Gentlewoman: Life in a Widow's Household in the Later Middle Ages* (Stroud, 1999).

Thomas, H. M., *Vassals, Heiresses, Crusaders and Thugs: The Gentry of Angevin*

Yorkshire, 1154–1216 (Philadelphia, PA, 1993).

Walker, Sue Sheridan (ed.), *Wife and Widow in Medieval England* (Michigan, 1993).

'Widow and Ward: The Feudal Law of Child Custody in Medieval England', in idem (ed.), *Wife and Widow in Medieval England* (Michigan, 1993), pp. 159–72.

Ward, Jennifer, *English Noblewomen in the Later Middle Ages* (London, 1992).

(ed.), *Women of the English Nobility and Gentry, 1066–1500* (Manchester, 1995).

Waugh, Scott L., *The Lordship of England: Royal Wardships and Marriage in English Society and Politics, 1217–1327* (Princeton, NJ, 1988).

Woolgar, Christopher M., *The Great Household in Late Medieval England* (London, 1999).

Wright, Susan M., *The Derbyshire Gentry in the Fifteenth Century*, Derbyshire Record Society, 8 (1983).

INDEX

A

abduction, 15, 22, 100, 108
abortion, *see* birth control
adoption, 15, 110
adultery, 8, 48, 53–4, 59, 80, 83, 89–90
Alexander III, pope, 12, 95
Alfegh, John, 106, 108
alimony, 83
Anglo-Saxons, 38, 76, 110–11
annuities, 88–90, 110, 121–2
annulment, 26, 28, 50, 67, 80–3, 125
    see also divorce
apprentices, 23–4, 73–4, 94–5, 97, 110, 122–3, 126
Aquinas, St Thomas, 18
Arthur, Prince, 108
Arundel, Richard, Earl of, 81–2
    see also Fitzalan, family
Augustine, St, 9, 15, 54, 60
Avranches, Compromise of, 10

B

banns, 24, 43–4, 46, 51, 89
baptism, 60–2
Bar, Joan of, 82
Beauchamp, family, 32
    see also Warwick, Richard
        Beauchamp, Earl of

Beaufort, Margaret, 98–9
Becket, St Thomas, 11
Berkeley, family, 119
    see also Beauchamp, family
betrothal, 9, 25, 35, 43–4, 46–7, 50, 81, 105
    see also handfasting; marriage
Betson, Thomas, 35
bigamy, 13–14, 44, 48, 50–1
birth control, 67–9
Black Death, *see* plague
Black Prince, Edward the, 31
Blanche, daughter of Henry de Grosmont, Duke of Lancaster, 31
Bohun, family, 21, 31, 97,107
    see also Hereford,
        Northampton and Essex,
        Humphrey, Earl of
Bonaventure, Thomasine, 97
Brent, family, 33, 75, 88
Brews, Margery, 35–6
Brown, family, 90–1, 105
Bryene, Alice de, 93–4
Burgh, Elizabeth de, 91–2, 100

C

Calle, Richard, 27–8, 55
Catesby, John, 33
Catherine of Aragon, 82

157